PIONEERS

of

St. Clair County, Michigan

PIONEERS

of

St. Clair County, Michigan

BRENDA L. WILLIAMS

THE
History
PRESS

Published by The History Press
Charleston, SC
www.historypress.com

Copyright © 2024 by Brenda L. Williams
All rights reserved

Portrait of Cummings Sanborn and Charlotte Fish Sanborn. Merchant Exchange Block and Military Street, 1908. *Images Courtesy of the Port Huron Museum.*
Portrait of Honorable Senator Omar Dwight Conger of Michigan, circa 1865–80. *Courtesy of the Library of Congress.*

First published 2024

Manufactured in the United States

ISBN 9781467155526

Library of Congress Control Number: 2024931891

CONTENTS

ACKNOWLEDGEMENTS

When I started writing a personal history blog about people from Michigan in 2017, I never imagined I would one day write a book for The History Press. I have so many people to thank for their generosity, patience and research assistance over the years. First and foremost, I wish to thank my acquisitions editor, John Rodrigue, and The History Press for giving me the opportunity to share these stories with you.

To my friend Jon Hardman, thank you for your interest in Henry McMorran and for conducting your "Thanks Henry" campaign on behalf of McMorran Arena many moons ago. It was your interest that sparked my curiosity about our hometown and started me on the path of learning about its rich history.

To my husband, Dennis, thank you for listening to all my historical findings and aiding in my research. A special thank-you to him for keeping the household running while I traveled on my research trips and spent countless hours locked away writing. Your endless support and belief in me never waivers. To my children, Matthew Sommerville, Emily Wilson and Miles Williams, thank you for allowing me to take time away from you to research and write.

To my best friend and mentor, Kenny Hamblin, thank you for taking me under your wing and providing me with the guidance and support I needed to start my blog. You provided me with a safe place to express myself. Our long talks about writing and marketing really keep me going on this journey.

To my cousin Lisa Stone, thank you for the encouragement and support over the years and for taking time out of your busy life to attend my historical presentations with me.

To my dear friend Susan Couch, thank you for listening, offering good advice about research pathways and assisting me in my research.

A special thanks to Janet Curtiss, the librarian at the St. Clair County Library in Port Huron, Michigan, for all your support, friendship and research assistance over the years. I would be lost without you.

A big thank-you to the following individuals for answering my questions, talking to me about Port Huron history and helping guide me in my research process: my friend and fellow research guru Cheri Smith Smigielski; my friend Angela C. Kelley; the members of the Facebook groups Photos of Port Huron's Past and Historic Port Huron and Surroundings; Vicky Armstrong, the president of the St. Clair County Genealogy and History Society; all of the staff at the Archives of Michigan; Veronica Campbell, the director of the Port Huron Museum, and her staff; and my newfound friends Erica and Elizabeth Wickings.

Last, but surely not least, I would like to thank my mother, Bonnie Lee McMillan, for sharing her love of history and books with me. My mother was a genius when it came to historical topics. She could tell you the history of almost anything. She was extraordinary and a true book nerd. Mom, you were my personal history teacher. I love you, and I wish you were here with me today to be a part of all of this.

INTRODUCTION

When I lost my mother suddenly in July 2013, it shook my world. I turned inward and started to evaluate my life choices. I realized some changes were in order, as I was not living an authentic life. This evaluation led me to give up my busy paralegal career at a big law firm in Dayton, Ohio. All that I knew then was that I was going to stay home for a little while, take care of my youngest son, Miles, and carve out some time to research and write a historical book on someone. I've always had a passion for history, genealogy and writing, and I wanted to explore being an at-home mom while taking the time to pursue my passion.

The two candidates I focused my research on were Virginia Kettering of Dayton, Ohio, and Henry McMorran of my hometown, Port Huron, Michigan. I eventually set my sights on my childhood home and chose to get to know Henry McMorran. My research journey started by browsing what I knew best, the law. As it turned out, Henry was a party to many lawsuits in his lifetime. From there, Henry provided me with my research path. He led me to the St. Clair County Library, the St. Clair County Probate Court, the St. Clair County Clerk of Courts, the Port Huron Museum, the Michigan Archives, the University of Michigan Library and the Chicago National Archives.

After I gathered enough material, I started my personal history blog, www.tappingroots.com, fully intent on sharing only stories about Henry's life. As I researched him, many other early pioneers of St. Clair County became known to me. Their names just kept reappearing. The stories in this book are just a few of the "rabbit holes" I wandered down while researching McMorran. I pursued these pioneers because their stories stuck with me, so I kept picking away at them. I have read and reread William Lee Jenks's book *St. Clair County, Michigan: Its History and Its People* many times over the past seven years. His work is truly a valuable resource. Jenks did a wonderful job researching and penning our early history, but in some instances, his work gives us more of a generalized overview of his subject matter. As I read his book, I kept asking myself, "Why?" Working in the law, the technique I used in my legal research was always to ask myself "Why?" repeatedly until I answered every question laid before me. There is no room for error in the law. If you miss something, you lose the case for your client. So, in my personal research, I find myself using this same strategy, which tends to give me more of a micro view of my subject.

My goal in writing personal history stories is to add to the historical work of those who came before me. My hope in writing this book is to give you a micro-level view into the lives of some of our early pioneers to gain a different perspective on our local history and the Pioneers of St. Clair County. I hope that by asking "Why?" we all can gain a clearer picture of some of the events that influenced their lives and made them the people they were. I simply wanted to know why Omar D. Conger lost his congressional seat, why James W. Sanborn was known as a mentor in the community, why Johnston and Co. went bankrupt, why the plaque on the exterior of the City Flats Hotel building was placed there and why J.P. Sanborn was known as King John. I hope you enjoy reading these stories as much as I enjoyed discovering them. Thank you for taking the time to read and appreciate our local history with me.

If you have a "why" of your own or a story you would like to share, please feel free to reach out to me. The best part about writing my blog and this book are the people I have met along the way: fellow researchers, writers, genealogists, family members of my subjects or those who just want to share a personal history story of their own. I would love to hear from you. You can contact me on my blog anytime: www.tappingroots.com.

EVOLUTION

The Southeast Corner of Military and Water Street in Port Huron, Michigan

When you consider the term *landownership*, what comes to mind? Do you immediately think *control* or *possession*? We have been taught to think of these two terms in correlation to land. However, under the law, landownership is only an existence of rights (like the right to sell, modify or prevent someone else from using land). So, what we own are rights, not the land. And while land itself is fixed, ownership is not. This leads one to think of the transitory nature of land over time and how the exercise of ownership rights influences its landscape.

The southeast corner of Military and Water Streets is historically significant to the city of Port Huron, because it links together the city's past and present. It is a reminder that our community was built on land that was originally home to Indigenous people. It is also a reminder of the first lot sold in Section 10 of our community, known to the area's earliest pioneers as the "Kerley Lot." In its ten thousand square feet space this lot held both worlds: the border of the Indian reservation and one of the first buildings of the pioneer settlement. Today, the bronze plaque on the City Flats Hotel building stands on the old Kerley Lot and pinpoints the reservation line. This memorial tablet was dedicated by the Ottawa Chapter of the Daughters of the American Revolution on June 15, 1931, to perpetuate the memory of the reserve. The building that displays the

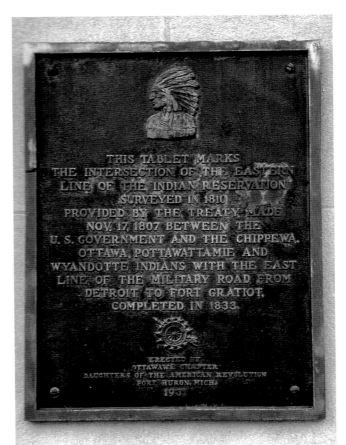

Right: A bronze plaque that marks the eastern line of the Indian reservation. *Author's image.*

Below: The boundary lines of the Township of Desmond from 1827 to 1837, as illustrated in *Economic and Social Beginnings of Michigan. Courtesy of the St. Clair County Library.*

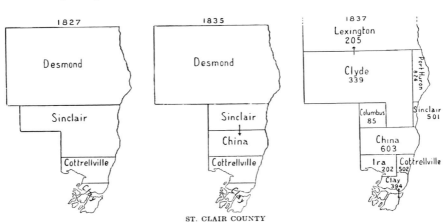

plaque has been reimagined and rebuilt various times over the years. In combination, the building and plaque commemorate one of Port Huron's most significant landmarks.

This story is a historical review of the Kerley Lot and its owners and how their influence colored its landscape. To tell its history, it is important to note the various names the area was known as historically. Before the 1820s, the Kerley Lot was part of the Township of Desmond. In 1821, as the boundaries of Wayne County changed, it became part of St. Clair County. After 1835, the Kerley Lot was part of the Village of Desmond, St. Clair County. After 1837, the Kerley Lot was part of the City of Port Huron. By the 1860s, the Kerley Lot was part of Lot 7, Block 93 of White's Plat, Port Huron, St. Clair County.

Joseph Watson

When William Hull came to Detroit as the newly appointed Governor of the Michigan Territory in July 1805, he wore many hats. In addition to his duties as governor, he was responsible for acting as the Commander in Chief and Superintendent of Indian Affairs. Hull quickly found himself in need of a clerk. To fill the position, he chose the son of his friend and confidant Elkanah Watson of Albany, New York. Joseph Watson would prove to be more than just the son of a famed Revolutionary War veteran. In the early years of the territory, most citizens of Detroit were of French origin. Being educated in France, Joseph spoke and wrote French fluently. Watson's attention to detail and reliability would become indispensable to Hull. From August 1806 until the time Hull surrendered Detroit, Watson served the Michigan Territory as Deputy Collector, Notary Public, Secretary to the Detroit Land Board, Deputy Marshall, City Registrar, Census Enumerator, Secretary of the Indian Department and Storekeeper, Justice of the Peace and Colonel of the Michigan Militia.

When the Michigan Territory was in its infancy, most of its land belonged to Indigenous people. The Port Huron area was known to them as Aamjiwnaang Territory, an area of land spanning both sides of the St. Clair River that stretched from Goderich, Ontario, Canada, to White Rock, Michigan. These peoples were part of the Anishinabek Nation, but the British and Americans referred to them as Chippewa. To effectuate colonial growth and settlement, President Thomas Jefferson issued Hull a commission to meet with the chiefs of all the local Indigenous Nations and negotiate a treaty for their land. Hull was given instructions to appoint a secretary to record the treaty articles. Hull chose Joseph Watson for the job. Both men were present for the signing of the Treaty of Detroit on November 17, 1807. This treaty not only ceded lands to the Americans, but it also created three local reservations for the Anishinabek people to reside on. One 1,200-acre reservation was located at the mouth of Black River in Port Huron. Two reservations were in Chesterfield, Michigan: one on Lake St. Clair (including Maconce's village) at the mouth of Riviere au Vase and one at the mouth of Salt Creek. Two of the Anishinabek chiefs who signed the treaty and made their home in Aamjiwnaang Territory were Little Thunder (Ne-ma-kay, Animikeence) and Old Macompte (Macquette-quet, Macounce, Maconce, Makongs). The nations who came to live on the three reservations created by the Treaty of Detroit would later be recognized by the U.S. government as one band, the Swan Creek and Black River Chippewa tribe. Prior to the Treaty of Detroit, these same two chiefs were also present and participated in the signing of Land Cession No. 7, which was a treaty executed with the British government in 1796. The land granted was located along the Chenail Ecarte, the wide channel of the St. Clair River Delta, at the mouth of the St. Clair River and Lake St. Clair. Today, the area is known as Sombra Township, Ontario. The lands ceded under these two treaties illustrate how large Aamjiwnaang Territory was and how irrelevant the United States–Canadian borderline was to local Indigenous Nations in the early years of the Michigan Territory. To these nations the land on both sides of the river was home.

After Hull negotiated the Treaty of Detroit, he wrote to Joseph's father, Elkanah, on November 30, 1807:

> *By this treaty for the consideration of fifty thousand dollars, I have purchased from the Indians more than five million acres, extending from Fort Defiance on the Miami, about two hundred and sixty miles upon that river, Lake Erie, the river Detroit, Lake St. Clair, the river St. Clair, and Lake Huron, comprehending all the rivers which fall into these waters, with all the islands in the same. The land is of excellent quality, and well suited for improvement. It is perhaps the most advantageous purchase the United States has ever made.*

THE WATSON PATENT:
MONTGATS AND THE KERLEY LOT

Before the War of 1812, in anticipation of a conflict with the British, Congress offered the incentive of 160 acres of land to any man who enlisted in the U.S. Army for five years or served the duration of a war. To keep the land warrants centralized, Congress proposed military tracts be created in the Michigan, Illinois and Louisiana Territories. After the war, applicants were given the liberty to choose a specific area in one of the designated territories to claim their land. In 1815, an unfavorable report issued by Surveyor General Edward Tiffin of the Michigan Territory made Congress reverse its prior decision and exclude the Michigan Territory from its designated military tract proposal list. Instead, it chose to substitute land in the Missouri Territory for military tract designation. This infuriated the new Michigan Territorial Governor, Lewis Cass. The report caused people in the country to have a negative view of Michigan, which would delay mass migration to Michigan for almost a decade, when Congress rescinded their decision and added Michigan back on the military tract sale list.

The steamboat *Walk-in-the-Water*, as illustrated in *Economic and Social Beginnings of Michigan*. *Courtesy of the St. Clair County Library.*

After the war, Joseph Watson was unable to retain a position in the Michigan Territory. So, he opened a military and general agency store in Washington, D.C., to assist veterans in obtaining their military land bounties. His wife, Sarah Witherell Watson, and his two young sons continued to reside in Detroit with her father, Judge James Witherell. Judge Witherell had served as a Supreme Court Justice under the Hull administration prior to the war. After the war, he was again appointed as a justice in the Cass administration. In 1818, Sarah Watson died, leaving her two sons in the care of her father in Detroit. In that same year, President James Monroe issued a Proclamation of Land Sales at Detroit to attract settlers to Michigan. In his proclamation, he designated sales of land in Wayne County to begin on the first Monday of September. Having designs of returning to the Michigan Territory to be with his two young sons and a desire to become a mercantile businessman, Joseph Watson boarded the new steamboat *Walk-in-the-Water* at Buffalo, New York, to travel to Detroit to purchase land. Coincidentally, the voyage is historically significant. *Walk-in-the-Water* was the first steamboat to ever travel on the waters of the Great Lakes, and Joseph was present on its maiden voyage. His sister-in-law, Mary Witherell Palmer, was also on the vessel. In a speech she gave to the Buffalo Historical Society in 1865, she remarked:

> *The first steamboat built on the upper lakes was named the* Walk-in-the-Water, *not only for its appropriateness, but for a chief of the Wyandot Indians, who lived with his band about 12 miles below Detroit....She made her trial trip in August, 1818....She reached Detroit about 9 o'clock Sunday morning Sept. 5th and as she ushered in a new era in the navigation of the upper lakes, her arrival was hailed with delight and announced by the firing of one gun, which custom was continued for many years.*

While in Detroit, Joseph purchased 80 acres in Section 10 in the Township of Desmond on September 19, 1818. At the time of his purchase, one house stood on the northeast corner of the Indian reservation near the present-day intersection of Water and Military Streets. The house belonged to local Metis chief, John Riley. At this time, the main populace in the area lived on the Fort Gratiot Miliary Reserve and the Indian reservation. When Joseph finally received his patent in 1821, according to William Lee Jenks in *St. Clair County, Michigan: Its History and Its People*, there were several French families living in shanties around the area. However, the only residents who were recorded as living in the Township of Desmond in 1821 were Anselm Petit and Zephaniah W. Bunce. Bunce purchased 98.35 acres of land in Section 28 and 80 acres in Section 29 on the same date Joseph Watson made his purchase. Petit made his land purchase in Section 11 a few years after them in June 1820.

Sometime after his purchase, Joseph employed Thomas Smith to plan out a town he called Montgats. Joseph would have been well acquainted with Mr. Smith. They both worked with the Detroit Land Board while under the Hull administration. Thomas Smith was a well-known Deputy Surveyor employed by the British government from 1799 until his death in 1833. He worked in connection with Judge Woodward and members of the Detroit Land Board to lay out the new city plan of Detroit. Mr. Smith resided in Sandwich, Ontario, Canada, which is present-day Windsor, Ontario. After the War of 1812, Smith continued to do survey jobs for the Michigan Territory until about 1821. The plat of Montgats was never recorded, so it is hard to pinpoint exactly when he performed the plat work for Joseph. This leaves us with a range somewhere between his purchase date in 1818 and his patent date in 1821.

In late 1827, six years after his purchase, Joseph Watson met with Michael Kerley in Detroit to discuss selling him a corner lot comprising ten thousand square feet in Montgats along the Black River. Michael was a Detroit fur trader at the time, so the corner lot that butted up against the Indian reservation would have been a prime location for him to expand his fur trade business beyond Detroit. Before Joseph would consent to the sale, he laid out two stipulations. He demanded Michael build a three-story warehouse or store as well as a wharf on the lot. In addition, he demanded absolute privilege to the ferry rights, with the ability to dock and transport goods on the wharf at no charge. As stipulated, Michael built the store and wharf sometime in 1827–28. We know this because Michael Kerley was a resident of Detroit when he initially met Joseph Watson. But in 1828, when he married his wife, Margaret Berthelet, he stated on his marriage certificate that he was living in the Township of Desmond. At this time, he was probably overseeing the construction of the store and wharf. Margaret was the daughter of Henry Berthelet, a prominent Detroit fur trader. She grew up on the old Labrosse farm, which is today part of the Corktown District of Detroit. Although Michael intended to go into the fur trade business in Montgats, he continued to retain a residence in Detroit.

In 1892, sixty-six-year-old Hiram Hamilton referred to a building erected on the Kerley Lot in his recollections to a reporter with the *Port Huron Times*. He recalled living in a hotel in 1828 called the Kerley House, which he remembered was kept by his father, Reuben Hamilton, and located on the banks of the Black River. He also recollected about a makeshift bridge across the Black River before the Military Street bridge was erected, "The only bridge across Black River at this time was located where the present iron structure is on Military Street and was made by arranging two boom poles, three or four feet apart, and placing them on wooden slabs fastened by wooden pins." His statement serves as proof that Micheal Kerley did build the store and wharf on the Watson property.

While we know business was being conducted at the store and wharf in 1828, Joseph held off another five years before selling Michael Kerley the property. During this period, they corresponded several times regarding the terms of sale. Eight years after Kerley built the wharf and store on the lot, Joseph finally conveyed to him a deed for a ten-thousand-square-foot lot located along the Indian reservation line and Black River on the southeast corner of present-day Military and Water Streets. The deed was dated March 27, 1835. The purchase price was $30. While Joseph sought to develop his town of Montgats and enter the mercantile business, his real estate business aiding veterans with their military bounty claims kept him so busy that it diverted his attention from his development plan. After 1819, the nature of his bounty land business changed dramatically, as taxes became due on military bounty land patentholders. Dealing with this issue took up most of his time. For the first three years after patent, Congress did not tax military bounty landowners. Patent holders, being hesitant to move to remote areas of Illinois, Ohio, Michigan and Arkansas, let their lands become tax-delinquent. This left land business owners like Joseph plenty of land to buy up at a reduced price. He would buy the land from the patent owner or have the military veteran issue him their power of attorney to handle the patent sale for them, pay the taxes and then resell it. In essence, Joseph became a land speculator of sorts. In Illinois alone, he acquired 134,240 acres of land through bounty land transactions. With all his attention on his land business, Joseph's vision for Montgats never materialized. Four months after Watson deeded the Kerley Lot, he sold the remaining acreage of Montgats to D.B. Harrington in July 1835 for $1,350. D.B. Harrington, in partnership with Judge Fortune T. White of New York, would later develop "White's Plat" in the City of Port Huron, which included the "Kerley Lot and the remaining Watson patent."

D.B. Harrington and Other Early Pioneers

In 1819, Daniel B. Harrington came through the Township of Desmond with his father, Jeremiah. He was twelve. They were on a fur trading expedition to Saginaw Bay from their hometown of Delaware, Ohio. In his memoirs to the Michigan Historical Society, D.B. recalled meeting Anselm Petit and Zephaniah W. Bunce on this journey. In the spring of 1822, Jeremiah moved his family to the area to settle permanently on a farm five miles from the mouth of Black River. Instead of staying on the farm with his father, D.B. sought employment in Detroit. In 1832, when Detroit experienced a cholera outbreak, he left the city and went to work for Joseph B. Comstock on Stony Creek in Oakland County. In the same year, John Howard and Francis P. Browning also left Detroit, bound for Port Huron to avoid the cholera outbreak, too. John Howard went into partnership with John Drew and built a sawmill on the north side of Black River. Francis P. Browning purchased six acres from John McNeil in the northeast section of Section 10 on the north side of the Black River to construct a steam mill. This section of land would become known as the Butler Plat, named after Charles Butler, a New York businessman and land speculator who visited the area in 1832 and purchased all the land on the tract, except for the six acres owned by Browning.

Between 1832 and 1833, the federal government built the military road from the Fort Gratiot Military Reservation to Detroit and the bridge over Black River. During its construction, a part of the road was built over the northeast corner of the Indian reservation near the John Riley homestead. After construction, this left a small piece of the reserve property on the east side of Military Street, next to the Kerley Lot. In 1833, Daniel B. Harrington returned home to his father's farm. This time, he went to work for Jonathan Burtch. Burtch had arrived in the area in 1828. It is written that he built a general store on the north side of the Black River, across from the Kerley Lot. In 1834, Francis P. Browning died of cholera. After his death, his business partners appealed to the Michigan Legislative Council to be incorporated into the Black River Steam Mill Company. Their request was granted in December. This company took over the Browning property, located west of the present site of the Seventh Street bridge. The principal owners of the business were Phineas Davis Jr., Enoch Jones, Bartlett A. Luce, Frederick H. Stevens, Edward Bingham, John Clark and Jonathan L. King.

In 1834, Cummings Sanborn bought land in Section 27 in Kimball Township and built a water mill on the Pine River in partnership with Larned

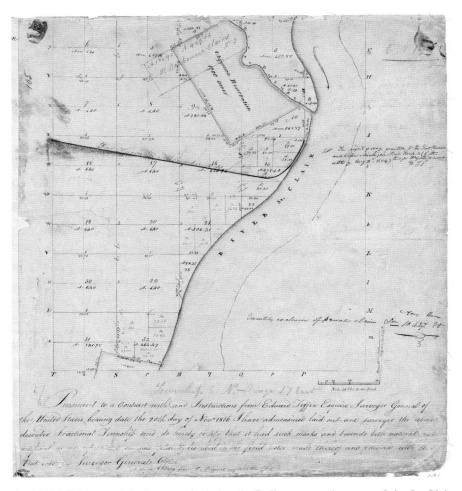

An 1818 Michigan original survey depicting the Indian reservation west of the St. Clair River, Township 6N, Range 17E. *Courtesy of the U.S. Department of the Interior, Bureau of Land Management.*

Smith, Horace Hall and Christopher Bartlett. By the spring of 1835, D.B. Harrington is noted, by William Lee Jenks in *St. Clair County, Michigan: Its History and Its People*, as running a business out of the wharf and store located on the Kerley Lot in partnership with his old boss, J.B. Comstock, and his brother Alfred. This timeframe coincides with Watson deeding the Kerley Lot to Michael Kerley in March 1835. This begs the question: Did Michael Kerley lease the wharf and store on his corner lot to D.B. Harrington and the Comstock brothers after he assumed ownership? Obviously, running a store was not the only aspiration D.B. Harrington had at the time. Land speculation and the platting of towns was also on his mind. During the same time frame, Jenks assigned D.B. Harrington to run a business at the store and wharf with the Comstock brothers; it has also been written D.B. Harrington visited his brother in Whitestown, New York, who was studying law under Judge Fortune White. During his visit, Harrington proposed a partnership with Judge White to buy land in Michigan. His proposal included Judge White funding the venture, with D.B. handling the platting and sale of the lots. For his services, D.B. asked to receive one-fourth of the proceeds of each lot sale. This account of D.B. Harrington meeting with Judge White in New York sometime in the spring of 1835 does coincide with the timing of his purchase of the Watson patent in July 1835. It would indicate he made the purchase after returning from New York. The fact that Jenks stated he was running a business on the Kerley Lot before he left for New York also makes one wonder if D.B. Harrington had advance warning Watson was interested in selling the remainder of his patented land and was the reason for his proposal to Judge White in the first place.

By 1836, local businessmen of the county were discussing the development of a local bank. While Michigan did not officially become a state until 1837, by the spring of 1836, it operated as a state and elected a state legislature. A petition for the incorporation of the bank was presented to the Michigan legislature on March 12, 1836, by Harrington's business partners, J.B. and Alfred Comstock, to be incorporated in the Village of Desmond. Thus, we know, by early 1836, the area around the Kerley Lot was known to the people in the community as the Village of Desmond.

A letter from Judge White to Harrington dated March 25, 1836, clearly evidences their relationship and desire to make their Village of Desmond the focal point of the county:

> *The bank charter that is applied for by the Palmer people works for me. It must be defeated if possible, but if it cannot, as your letter intimates, then if the location is to be fixed by the directors we must by all means secure a majority of the stock so that proper directors shall be chosen. I will be ready with the requisite funds. But do not mistake directors for commissioners, who are to locate it. In all charters commissioners are appointed to distribute the stock, etc. and then the directors are chosen by the stockholders, but let it be which way it will. You will see that everything will depend on having proper commissioners, for they are to distribute stock, and in doing that they can give a majority to stockholders who will be opposed to Desmond; we*

must make every effort to sustain Desmond. Money for the stock shall not be wanting, you may calculate on it.

Instead of being fixed in the Village of Desmond, as Judge White and D.B. Harrington hoped for, the bank charter was granted and placed in the City of Palmer, which is today St. Clair, Michigan. The first commissioners of the bank included Charles Kimball; Samuel Ward; John Clark; H.N. Monson, a representative of Thomas Palmer; Cummings Sanborn; D.B. Harrington; and Ralph Wadhams.

By 1837, D.B. Harrington's community was renamed Port Huron and was showing signs of economic growth. There were at least two lumbering mills in the general vicinity, a general store and the store and wharf located on the Kerley Lot.

THE INDIAN RESERVATION AND WHITE'S PLAT

The decades that followed the War of 1812 had devastating effects on the Indigenous people living along the Canadian and American border on the St. Clair River. The rush of white settlers to the area after the opening of the Erie Canal forced many land cession treaties. In addition, by 1830, Indigenous people in the United States faced the threat of removal to lands west of the Mississippi. While those living in Michigan were never ordered to move, a series of treaties from 1833 to 1837 contained language that requested their removal.

The Black River and Swan Creek Chippewa band located on the Indian reservation in Port Huron found themselves restricted to reserve land, which was too small to retain their traditional way of life of fishing, hunting and gathering. As the prime timber in the area fed the development of the Port Huron community, encroachment on the reserve became a problem. In late 1835, members of the Ottawa and Chippewa tribes wrote to Lewis Cass, then the Secretary of War, about their willingness to sell some of their land while maintaining their desire to stay in Michigan, "It is a heartrending thought to our simple feelings to think of leaving our native country forever, the land where our forefathers lay thick in the earth."

On May 9, 1836, in Washington, D.C., four chiefs of the Swan Creek and Black River Chippewa bands in Port Huron and Chesterfield ceded their reservations created under the Treaty of Detroit. Under this treaty, the tribes were to be given the payment from the sale of the lands, minus the costs of survey and sale by the United States. They were also offered 8,320 acres or thirteen sections of land west of the Mississippi. Two of the chiefs who signed the treaty in Washington were related to the chiefs who had signed Land Cession No. 7 in 1796 and the Treaty of Detroit in 1807. Esh-ton-o-quot, or Clear Sky, who is also known historically as Maconse, Maconce, Machonce, Makonse, Makons and Francis McCoonse was the son of Old Macompte; and Nay-gee-zhig, or Driving Clouds, was the nephew of Annimekance, or Little Thunder. Nay-gee-zhig was the son of Mishikinaibik, also known as Great Snake or Black Snake, and the grandson of Mashkeash.

In 1837, the chiefs who signed the treaty in Washington, D.C., went to look at lands west of the Mississippi and grew hesitant about leaving their homeland. In early 1837, members of the Ottawa and Chippewa tribes again wrote to Washington, this time to newly elected President Martin Van Buren, professing, "You know we obtained our land from the Great Spirit. He made it for us who are Indians. When we die, we expect to rest on this land. We do not have mind to remove to a distant land." Later that year, Nay-gee-zhig also wrote to President Van Buren, detailing his concerns about the condition of the Indian reservation in Port Huron. His letter, dated November 2, 1837, stated:

> *In the first place we complain, that since the arrangement we made with you, our Great Father at Washington, authorizing you to dispose of our Reserve of twelve hundred acres of land for our benefit, which was then well wooded with a valuable forest of the best pine and oak trees, that a large and greater part of said trees have been cut and carried off last winter by the citizens of the United States, residing at the Village at Black River, and has been by them converted into several sand cords of steamboat wood, and the materials of a new vessel built there last winter have been taken off of our said Reserve. As we had given up the possession to our Father, we had no authority to prevent the depredation, we therefore, pray our Great Father to give orders to the United States Agent to enumerate us for the said depredations, as our said land will not now sell for more than one half of what it was worth when we gave you the authority to sell it for our benefit.*

To pen and send this letter to the President, Nay-gee-zhig had to travel from Port Huron to Detroit, where the Superintendent of Indian Affairs Office was located. This trip is about seventy miles one way. In addition, once he reached Detroit, he had to find a white man who would be willing

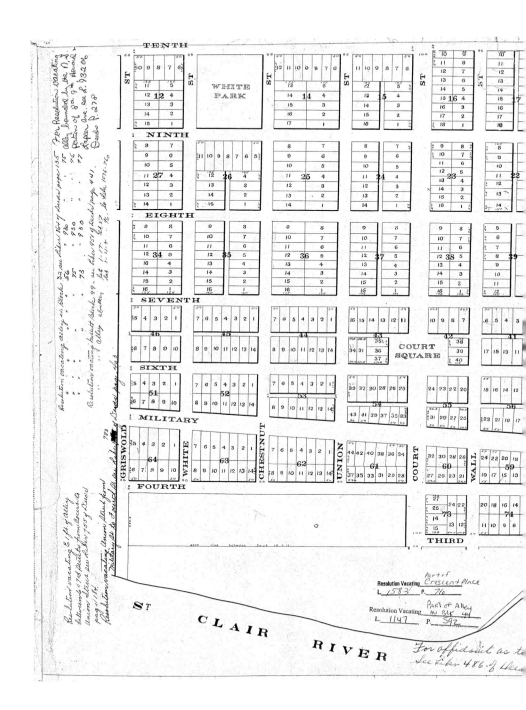

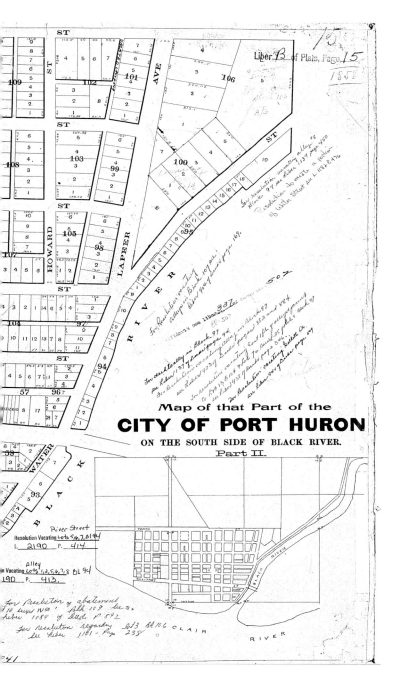

White's Plat, Port Huron, Michigan. *Courtesy of the St. Clair County Register of Deeds.*

to acknowledge his letter as dictated to the agent at the Indian affairs office and deliver it to the President in Washington, D.C., for him. Since James V.S. Riley, the father of Metis chief John Riley, was visiting Detroit at the time, he agreed to be that man.

On May 22, 1839, the United States put the Indian reservation land on sale. One of the first purchasers that day was Judge White. He bought all the acreage of Lot/Tract 2 next to the Watson Patent in Section 10. This purchase allowed him to extend the original borders of White's Plat stretching the area east to Third Street and south to Griswold Street.

After the sale of their reservations in Port Huron and Chesterfield, the Swan Creek and Black River bands were still hesitant to move to Kansas. On July 6, 1839, Henry Schoolcraft, the Michigan Superintendent of Indian Affairs, responded to their concerns in a letter to Chief Francis McCoonse:

Ever since your visit to Washington for the purpose of selling your lands your Great Father has called on you Makonse, as a man of sense who is capable of managing the affairs of his red children on Swan Creek and Black River. And it is to you that he now addresses himself that you may give your chiefs and people right counsel. The late sale of your lands puts the white people in possession of them and you can no longer remain on them in prosperity or safety. There are no longer any animals on these lands to hunt and every meal you get costs you money. White men sell your corn and clothes and the worst of all things, liquor in hopes to get their pay out of your annuities. And when you are poor and have no money to pay them, they sue you. The records of our Courts prove this. Why should you remain here? You have better lands and in a fine climate west of the Mississippi where you can raise plenty of corn and hogs and cattle without cutting hay to keep them through the winter. There are also many animals for you to hunt in the woods and prairies and fish in the streams. There are also forests of trees as you know and have yourself seen which you can cut down to build houses and make fences. There is but little snow on these and you will not want as many blankets or so much woolen clothing. One can plough upon the prairies without labor of clearing and grubbing them. Half the labor you bestow here will be double rewarded. And if you remove to those lands secured to you by you cannot fail to become happy if you are industrious and temperate. Your letter addressed to me at Washington last Fall offering to go west was received by me at Washington and laid before the President. He has approved it. He has provided money to send you west and appointed Agents and Interpreters to take you there and see to your comfort by the way. There will also be a physician to attend to the sick, tents to sleep in, and wagons for women and children after you reach Westport. While you live in Michigan, white men will treat you ill, furnish you the means of intoxication and trample on your rights. In the Indian Territory to which you are going, no white men are allowed to come and settle. It is an offence against the law for white men to go over the Indian lines and no whiskey can be taken to poison and degrade the Indians. You will govern your bands and each band will send chiefs to a general council and the general council will make laws for all the Indians. And the Indian nations will there become powerful, free and happy. Each one who agrees to go will have his name put down on a roll.

With no recourse to avoid removal, Chief McCoonse left Michigan with about sixty-four of his people in late 1839 to live in Franklin County, Kansas. By early 1840, according to Henry Schoolcraft, Nay-kee-shick was living on the Canadian side of the St. Clair River on the Sarnia Reserve in Ontario, Canada, with most of his people.

The Kerley Lot Becomes the Merchants Exchange Block

The Kerley Lot had many owners between 1835 and 1837. On December 2, 1835, Michael Kerley sold his ten-thousand-square-foot lot to Elihu L. Hannah and Stephen V. Thornton for $1,000. In 1837, Hannah sold his portion of the lot to Peter Brakeman for $1,100, and Peter turned around and sold it to John H. Westbrook for $1,200. Thornton then sold his portion of the lot to John H. Westbrook the same year for $1,500. By May 1837, Westbrook owned the entirety of the lot until Thornton decided to repurchase the west part of the lot from him for $1,500. The 1840 assessment roll for Port Huron shows Hannah and Thornton did business at the wharf and store on the Kerley Lot, even though Westbrook and Thornton owned the land they conducted their business on.

In 1841, Cummings Sanborn moved from Kimball Township to Port Huron with his wife, Charlotte (Fish) Sanborn. Charlotte was the daughter of Allen Fish Sr. and Clarissa Burch. In Port Huron, Cummings went into the mercantile business with his nephew Martin S. Gillett. Their business was known as Sanborn, Gillett and Co. Martin was the son of Sanborn's sister

Mary Sanborn Gillett and Israel Gillett of Hartford, Vermont. In 1843, Gillett purchased the east half of the Kerley Lot from Westbrook. In 1846, Cummings Sanborn purchased the west half from Thornton for $1,200. Together, Cummings and Gillett rebuilt a two-story wooden building on the site. In addition to his business with Gillett, Cummings continued to operate his mill in Kimball Township, and he built a steam sawmill with John Howard and John L. Beebe on the north side of Griswold Street in 1849. In June 1849, Cummings sold a cord of his portion of the Kerley Lot to Judge White for $1, and Judge White turned around and sold it to Alvah Sweetser and James W. Sanborn for $1,000. A cord is a measurement of real property equal to .0003673 acres. James W. Sanborn had come from Falmouth, Maine to Michigan to work for his uncle Charles Merrill, Abner Coburn and Joseph L. Kelsey. For the first few years, he managed the 25,000 acres of pineland in St. Clair and Sanilac Counties the three men had purchased. In 1845, James started into business for himself with his brother-in-law, Alvah Sweetser. Alvah was married to James's sister, Mary Sanborn. In 1847, they came together to Port Huron. Their principal businesses were lumber, merchandise and real estate. James W. Sanborn already had a family member established in business in Port Huron, which would prove helpful. He and Cummings Sanborn were second cousins.

In June 1851, Sweetser and Sanborn sold a piece of the cord to Martin Gillett. A portion of the property description reads, "Beginning at a point on the north line of Water Street thirty-eight feet westerly from the west line of land owned by Cummings Sanborn said point being the center of the division wall that separates the cellar now occupied by Martin S. Gillett from the cellar now occupied and owned by the said Sweetser and Sanborn running from thence westerly on the north line of said Water Street to the east line of Military Street." This description tells us that in June 1851, Alvah Sweetser, James Sanborn, Martin Gillett and Cummings Sanborn each owned different sections of the building on the Kerley Lot.

By 1851, many different companies were operating in the building. H.J. Bockius rented space from Martin Gillett and operated a shoe store. Sweetser and Sanborn operated their real estate business there. Allen and Henry Fish, Charlotte (Fish) Sanborn's brothers, ran the storefront for Cummings and Gillett. Omar Conger and William Bancroft also operated their law office on the upper floor of the wooden building. In 1852, Cummings Sanborn died, and his interest in his businesses passed to Allen and Henry Fish.

In 1853, the temperance movement and the prohibition of alcohol were intense topics at public meetings that roused strong emotions on both sides of the debate. Martin Gillett and Alvah Sweetser were strong advocates in support of the temperance movement. As a result, their building on the Kerley Lot was set on fire and destroyed in March 1854. The local sheriff offered a $500 reward for information leading to the arrest of the person(s) responsible for the fire. This led to the arrest of two men, one of whom was convicted after a second trial. Thankfully, all the merchants in the building had insurance and were able to move to other locations and continue in business until a new building was established on the site.

When Cummings Sanborn died, his widow, Charlotte, was to receive $5,000 and all household furnishings under his will. After the fire, on April 5, 1854, Charlotte Fish Sanborn petitioned the probate court to ask for her portion of the estate to be set off. She was anxious to have money to sustain her while she was waiting for the final settlement of his estate. In her pleading to the court, she specifically requested her homestead, valued at $1,080 on Lots 29 and 31 and the east half of Lot 22 in Block 55 of White's Plat and the business property "to include the store lot and wharf lately occupied by Mr. A&H Fish, known as a part of the Kerley Lot, except a vacant strip heretofore sold and conveyed to Mr. Sweetser and Sanborn." The business property on her petition was appraised at $2,000.

On April 8, 1854, she revised her petition to include "the insurance money due and coming for the destruction of the store lately, thereon and destroyed by fire and which money is also assigned to me as part thereof." The court granted her request for the homestead and business property along with any insurance money. In July 1854, Charlotte sold her interest in the Kerley Lot to Sweetser and Sanborn for $580. She married James W. Sanborn in June 1855. It was the second marriage for both. Also in 1855, Martin Gillett, Alvah Sweetser and James W. Sanborn built a new four-story brick building on the site of the Kerley Lot. It became known as the Merchant Exchange Block. The contractor was Henry N. Wright.

NEIGHBORS

The early pioneers who shared ownership of the original Kerley Lot also shared a neighborhood. Cummings Sanborn's home was located on Military Street on the south half of the block between Wall and Court Streets, close to where the Kerr Albert Office Supply building stands today. When Charlotte (Fish) Sanborn died, she left a life estate for her sister, Fanny Spaulding, to live

The north half of the west side of Sixth and Pine Streets, 2022. This was the former site of the James W. Sanborn home. *Author's image.*

in Charlotte's home until Fanny's death. Fanny was widowed and had young children. The home was to pass to Charlotte's son, Herbert Sanborn, upon Fanny's death. Fanny was the mother of early pioneer Edgar Spaulding. The Spaulding family lived in the Cummings Sanborn home until 1881, when Herbert Sanborn took possession and moved in with his family. John Miller was their neighbor. He lived in the north half of the block. Miller's home still stands on Military Street, across the street from the Harrington Hotel. The Harrington Hotel stands on the old D.B. Harrington homestead.

James W. Sanborn lived a few blocks away on the north half of the block on the west side of Sixth Street between Pine and Wall Streets, which is now a parking lot. Martin Gillett lived on the south half of the same block in a brick dwelling that is now occupied by Our Savior Lutheran Church, located across from the American Legion Hall.

Most people associate James W. Sanborn with the home that still stands on the corner of Seventh and Union Streets at 1305 Seventh Street today. However, this home was built after James's death, sometime in 1875, by his third wife, Mehitabel Sanborn. Alvah Sweetser lived in a large frame

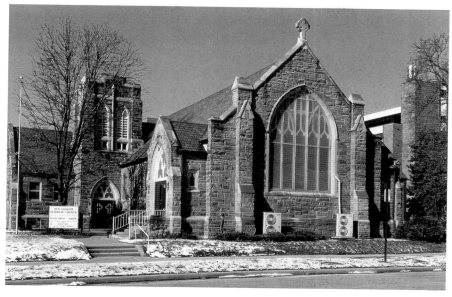

Our Savior Lutheran Church on the southwest corner of Sixth and Pine Streets, Port Huron, Michigan, the former site of the Martin Gillet home. *Author's image.*

The old Mehitabel Sanborn home on the corner of Seventh and Union Streets, Port Huron, Michigan, 2023. *Author's image.*

house on the southwest corner of Military and Pine Streets. In 1910, Elk Lodge No. 343 built the Elks lodge on this property. This building has been changed since 1910, but you can still visualize the lower half of the Elks temple on that corner today.

The Merchant Exchange Block

The first businesses in the new brick block were William Wastell's drugstore, Wallace and Gibson's dry goods store, E.R. Sweetser's store, Sweetser and Sanborn's general store and real estate business, A. & H. Fish's general store, W.B. and J. Hibbard's lumber store and Hull and Boyce's hardware store. Later, E.R. Sweetser, who was Alvah Sweetser's brother, joined the Sweetser and Sanborn business. W.B. and J. Hibbard also operated a lumber mill. They eventually sold the mill to John and Henry Howard. This mill would become known as the Howard Mill, which operated on the north side at the mouth of the Black River, where it meets the St. Clair River.

In later years, J.P. Sanborn operated a general store in the building. J.P. Sanborn was James W. Sanborn's nephew. Over various periods, other occupants of the building included the Port Huron Post Office, the *Port Huron Daily Times*, the *Sunday News*, Patterson Music Company and Foster Brothers shoe store. The earliest directory for Port Huron, published in

Merchant Exchange Block. *Image courtesy of the Port Huron Museum.*

1870, was printed in the Merchant Exchange Block. In that directory, the street numbers for the block are 3–5 Military Street and 37–45 Water Street. The present numbers are 810–812 Military Street and 407–415 Water Street.

The Wastell Block

By the late 1880s, the building had become known as the Wastell Block. This is probably because all the original owners, James W. Sanborn, Cummings Sanborn, Martin Gillett and Alvah Sweetser, had passed away by then, and William Wastell continued operating his drugstore business there. J.P. Sanborn continued to operate his offices out of the building, too. While J.P. Sanborn and William Wastell never owned an interest in the building, members of their family inherited ownership through the original owners. In William Wastell's case, his wife, Ann Gillett, eventually owned a portion of the building. Ann was the daughter of Martin Gillett. In 1865, when Gillett died, his interest passed to his wife, Eliza Gillett. When she became too old to care for herself, she deeded her interest in the property to Ann. In J.P. Sanborn's case, he acted as the trustee of the James W. Sanborn and Mary J. Sweetser estates and maintained the ownership interest for the members of the Sanborn family named in their trusts, which included James's widow, his children, his siblings and his grandchildren.

Business space in the Wastell Block was not the only thing William Wastell and J.P. Sanborn shared. They were also family by marriage. They were brothers-in-law. William Wastell was the son of Reverend W.P. Wastell, who was the pastor of the First Congregational Church in Port Huron from 1853 to 1855. William's sister Mary Wastell married J.P. Sanborn in 1855. The Gillett, Wastell and Sanborn families were all active members in the First Congregational Church.

During this period, the building was also used as a space for social club meetings and community gatherings and was sometimes referred to as Wastell's Hall. William and Ann Wastell eventually moved into the Gillett homestead on Sixth Street to take care of Ann's aging mother. William Wastell passed away in 1898. In 1902, Ann fell from a streetcar on Huron Avenue. The accident left her an invalid until her death in 1904. Fearing she would pass away before her mother, leaving her mother with no one to care for her, Ann signed over the deeds to the Gillett home and her interest in the

Wastell Block to her son Fred a few days before her death. She also made a will that bequeathed her estate to her two sons, Fred and John. She named Fred the executor. When her will was admitted for probate, Fred disclosed his mother had signed over the real estate, which was the only property of value in her estate, so he could provide for the care of his grandmother. John sued Fred to have the deeds declared invalid, and a long court battle ensued. Their grandmother passed away in 1912, and John dropped the lawsuit against his brother in 1916.

St. Clair County Savings Bank

In 1895, the St. Clair County Savings Bank was erected next to the Wastell Block on the north side of the building, closest to the Black River. This was possible because Henry McMorran and his brother-in-law, Nelson Mills, had acquired the Sanborn Sweetser portion of the lot in 1892. They purchased it from J.P. Sanborn, while he was still acting as Trustee of the Mary S. Sweetser and James W. Sanborn estates. The bank was built of red stone and brick at the cost of $9,000. By 1909, the St. Clair County Savings Bank needed more space and wanted to build a new bank on the site. E.F. Percival, who was a stockholder in the bank, liked the structure, so he negotiated a deal to buy it. He had it moved stone by stone to the southeast corner of Military and Pine Streets. The building still sits there today. He operated a real estate office out of it until he died. In the mid-1950s until about 1990, it housed Askar Shain's photography studio.

After E.F. Percival moved the old bank, the St. Clair County Savings Bank built their new bank on the property next to the Wastell Block. In June 1913, a fire broke out in the Wastell Block, which damaged three floors of the building. At the time of the fire, the only businesses in the building were the Palms Café and Foster Brothers shoe store. It was becoming apparent to the community that the old Wastell Block needed renovation.

Michigan National Bank

By the early 1900s, many of the banks in Port Huron had begun consolidating and joining the Federal Reserve System. In 1911, the Commercial Bank and

Left: The St. Clair County Savings Bank building, Port Huron, Michigan, 2018. *Author's image*.

Below: A postcard of St. Clair County Savings Bank, circa 1910. *Author's image*.

the Port Huron Savings Bank consolidated. In 1917, the St. Clair County Savings Bank joined the Federal Reserve System, and then the Commercial Bank followed suit, joining in 1918. That same year, the Commercial Bank and the St. Clair County Savings Bank consolidated to become the Federal Commercial and Savings Bank. After the consolidation, a new bank building was proposed on the site where the St. Clair County Savings Bank stood.

Because the St. Clair County Savings Bank was already operating in a building next to the old Wastell Block and the Wastell Block needed repair, the members of both banks decided the site of their proposed new bank building should be on the lot that held the old Wastell Block building. This way, the bank would be in possession of the whole lot. The shareholders of the bank asked E.F. Percival to begin talks with the owners of the old Wastell Block building to purchase it. The only store remaining in the old Wastell Block building at the time was the Foster Brothers shoe store. In 1920, the bank was able to negotiate the purchase with the owners who were the two Wastell brothers, Henry McMorran and Nelson Mills.

In 1927, the Federal Commercial and Savings Bank began demolishing the Wastell Block. It took the building down in parts, starting with the Military Street side of the building. The upper part of the next section was then taken off, and a new roof was placed over the store located at

The Michigan National Bank building, Port Huron, Michigan, 2020. *Author's image*.

413 Water Street. The bank used this section as a temporary accounting department while it constructed the new building. The contractor in charge of the demolition said, "The floor joints are 2-and-½-by-12 timbers, all clear pine. Such material cannot be obtained today."

In 1928, the new bank building was open for business. In 1936, the Federal Commercial and Savings Bank merged with the First National Trust and Savings Bank. In 1940, the Michigan National Bank was founded in Lansing, Michigan, by the consolidation of six Michigan banks. One of these banks was the First National Trust and Savings Bank of Port Huron. This is why the bank building bears the name Michigan National Bank today.

REMEMBER

From its beginnings as Aamjiwnaang Territory to the City Flats Hotel site today, this historical review of the southeast corner of Military and Water Streets reminds us of the transitory nature of land and the influence that owners can have on its landscape. In 1931, when the DAR unveiled the bronze tablet on the Federal Commercial and Savings Bank building, as it was known during that time, Mrs. McDonald said it best,

> *It is a privilege to be an American, to live restlessly and expectantly just to wait for what is around the corner for us. As we stand on this historical spot, we have this beautiful building, a modern achievement. Automobiles and busses whirl by on the concrete. I pause to look back to the time of which Mr. Jenks has spoken today. Here the Indians, ill-treated, and despised, trod daily through the virgin forest. Today civilization has given us a new place and new scene. I am thankful for the sacrifice which was made by those who gave in sorrow that we might have in peace and joy.*

In tune with that feeling, it must be said that we should always remember and acknowledge those who walked before us, for they all have a story to tell and a lesson to teach us. May you always be grateful and mindful as you pass by this very special corner that we all, past and present, claim in our community. For it serves as a reminder of those who gave up their precious home so that we could have ours.

2

THE TIES THAT BIND

*P*ort Huron is a small town that originated from the lumber, water transportation and the railroad industries. But at its core, the people and the community are the heart of the city. This is true yesterday and today. When you grow up in a small town, commonalities instinctively form between the people you live with, and connections are made that bind the community together. This is a story about a pioneer banker and how his life experiences impacted the history of another local pioneer family.

LOCAL BANKING IN PORT HURON

By 1856, a young Port Huron progressed as a lumbering community, reaching a population of 3,300. As the population and lumber business grew, so did the need for a local bank. State regulations at the time made it difficult to incorporate a state bank. There were also a variety of different currencies that existed in the economy. Gold and silver coins constituted hard money and were known as specie. Banknotes were a prevalent form of exchange between buyers and sellers. Banknotes issued from out-of-state banks, and foreign coins were also being used in the local economy.

A John Johnston and Co. and John Miller and Son advertisement, as illustrated in the *Merchant's and Banker's Almanac*, 1870. *Courtesy of the Internet Archive.*

State banks retained the privilege of issuing banknotes in lieu of specie. However, they could only issue banknotes up to the amount of specie they had on hand. Private banks became commonplace in rural areas to replace the access gap created by the limited number of state banks in Michigan. Private banks were not subject to state regulation and audit. Because of this, they could not issue their own banknotes. However, they could take in banknotes in exchange for specie. They also paid specie in exchange for land warrants and mortgages using state banknotes and foreign coins. In doing so, they provided liquidity to a locality by increasing the potential pot of money in the areas where they operated. Many private banks worked in conjunction with a correspondent bank, usually one out of a major city like New York.

John Miller and Co. and John Johnston and Co.

The first private bank in Port Huron was started in 1856 by Cyrus Miles and William Bancroft. Their correspondent banks were Duncan, Sherman and Co. in New York and Farmers and Mechanics Bank in Detroit. This firm operated for a few months before Bancroft retired. John Miller took his place, and the bank was operated as John Miller and Co. In 1865, John Johnston came to Port Huron from St. Clair to open another private bank. He partnered with W.C. Green under the firm name Johnston and Green. John Johnston was also engaged in the lumbering business with James Beard, Elijah R. Haynes and F.H. Vanderburg in Alcona Township, Michigan, under the firm Johnston Haynes and Co. In 1866, W.C. Green withdrew from the banking firm. In 1867, John Johnston reorganized the bank under the name John Johnston and Co. The directors and stockholders included Johnston, John L. Woods, James W. Sanborn, I.D. Carleton and H.G. Barnum. Their correspondent banks were Henry Clews and Co. in New York and the National Insurance Bank in Detroit.

In 1868, Cyrus Miles retired from John Miller and Co. John Miller took his son John E. Miller Jr. into the partnership, and the firm became known as John Miller and Son.

A New Banking Enterprise: The First National Bank

In 1863, the first National Banking Act was passed to establish a national currency that was backed by government securities. This gave the government the ability to sell war bonds and securities to help fund the Civil War effort. It also placed a higher capital requirement on national banks and made them subject to regulation by the federal government. After the Civil War, more National Banking Acts were passed to make state banks convert to national banks. By placing a 10 percent tax on banknote payments not issued by national banks, many private and state banks converted. In response to these new acts and the increased population in Port Huron, John Miller held a meeting in October 1870 with his competitor John Johnston to organize their two private banks into one national bank. Because the standards required a large amount of capital, he also invited the city's most wealthy men to the table. At the meeting, all of the bank members from both banks agreed to reorganize and create a new bank. The new stockholders in the venture were D.B. Harrington, John Miller, Henry Howard, James Goulden and O'Brien J. Atkinson (two hundred shares each); Samuel S. Ward (one hundred shares); and John Johnston (three hundred shares). After determining each member's stock distribution, the men elected themselves directors and adjourned.

A few days later, they reconvened to elect the new officers of the bank. The most important office was cashier. This position was one that needed to be filled by someone who had experience running a bank. That left John Miller and John Johnston vying for the position. The men held three separate votes. During the first and second vote for cashier, John Johnston received three votes from his fellow peers. During the third vote, O'Brien Atkinson received the highest number of votes. All the members knew Atkinson had no intention of acting as cashier, because he maintained a busy legal practice in town. Due to the irregularities in the votes for cashier, the members decided to discontinue the vote for the day and decide the matter later. They turned their attentions to a vote for President. A unanimous vote was tallied, and the office of President was given to D.B. Harrington. After the vote for President, the members convened the meeting.

The members went about the business of organizing the new bank. The next meeting of the shareholders took place on January 10, 1871, at which time, they again elected themselves directors. They voted again for president and cashier. D.B. Harrington was voted President for a second time, and John Miller was voted in as cashier. In August 1871, they met and elected Henry Howard, Vice-President and John E. Miller, Assistant Cashier. They organized the capital of the bank at $100,000. The bank began business in September 1871 as the First National Bank of Port Huron.

Having failed to be elected cashier, John Johnston pulled out of the venture and decided to reorganize John Johnson and Co. He parted ways with the members of the First National Bank, selling 260 shares of his stock to Miron Williams (60 shares), John Miller (150 shares) and Fred L. Wells (50 shares). On the same day, Samuel S. Ward sold his 50 bank shares to D.B. Harrington. This gave John Miller and D.B. Harrington equal shares in the bank, each retaining 250. John Johnston must have had a significant reason to walk away from the First National Bank deal, because his private bank at the time was in a vulnerable state. Just before John Miller asked him to join their two private banks together, one of Johnston's wealthiest shareholders, James W. Sanborn, died. His death was a significant loss for the bank. It prompted shareholders I.D. Carleton and James L. Woods to sell their shares and withdraw from John Johnston and Co. While Johnston found new partners in H.G. Barnum and Fred L. Wells, joining the new venture was later proven to have been in his best interest.

THE BEGINNING OF TROUBLE FOR JOHN JOHNSTON AND CO.

By May 1872, trouble began brewing between the two banking houses, John Johnston and Co. and the First National Bank. For many years, John Johnston's bank had been the holder of the city funds. In 1872, John Miller was acting Mayor, and his fellow banking partner O'Brien Atkinson was an alderman on the city council. Being shareholders in First National Bank together, Miller and Atkinson devised a scheme to remove the city funds to their bank. To counter them, John Johnston ran for City Treasurer but lost the nomination to another Republican, Antwine Marontate.

Under the charter laws of the city, the treasurer retained custody and control of all the city funds, and it was active practice for the treasurer to decide where the city funds were held. It was also active practice for the treasurer to declare a bond of $20,000 and disclose his bondsman to the members of the city council before assuming his official duties. His bondsman was usually a friend or person in the community who vouched his own money on behalf of the elected treasurer as a form of insurance.

On May 7, 1872, Antwine Marontate appealed to the city council to accept or reject his official bond. The city council members refused to install him until a resolution brought forward by Alderman O'Brien Atkinson was voted on. This resolution called for the city funds to be moved from John Johnston and Co. and placed in the First National Bank. Atkinson moved to allow competition to dictate where the funds were held moving forward. The amount of cash to be deposited was $11,000. The resolution was passed.

A few days after the meeting, it was discovered that the funds had already been removed to the First National Bank before the adoption of the resolution. This caused a rift between Democrats and Republicans in the city. The *Port Huron Times* called for the removal of Alderman Atkinson, citing his interest in the bank conflicting with his interest in holding public office. On May 23, 1872, Antwine Marontate again appealed to the city council to accept or reject his official bond, and it was reported after the meeting that Atkinson had made a nominal sale of his stock in the bank and resigned as Vice-President.

The "Long" and "Short" of it is a general "Bust" up in the "Street."

Financial Panic of 1873, Thomas Nast cartoon. *Courtesy of the Everett Collection/Shutterstock.com.*

The city moved on. Marontate was bonded, and the funds remained in the First National Bank. In September 1872, John Johnston was nominated for County Treasurer by the Board of Supervisors to fill the vacant position after the death of the current County Treasurer. Johnston accepted the position, and the county funds were deposited into his banking firm. John Johnston held this position for many years.

By October 1872, a smear campaign against Johnston's bank began to circulate in the community. It was rumored he operated a type of speculating bank, making him untrustworthy. Despite the efforts of the city councilmen and members of the First National Bank to discredit Johnston, John Johnston and Co. remained in operation.

THE PANIC OF 1873

On September 18, 1873, a panic on Wall Street set in motion the suspension of many U.S. banks. The panic started in Europe when investors started selling off their investments in American enterprise, especially railroad projects. Railroads, being new inventions, were popping up across the country. These companies borrowed money at an accelerated rate to get cash to build their roads. Many banks sold bonds on the market to fund them. Some banks were heavily invested in railroad bonds themselves. By May 1873, some stock markets in Europe had crashed. Europeans stopped buying railroad bonds. On September 18, when European bondholders started selling their bonds and flooding the market, one of the biggest banks in the United States, Jay Cooke and Co., went bankrupt. This bank had invested a lot of money in the Northern Pacific Railway.

The bankruptcy of this firm started a panic, and people in New York went to their banks in droves to withdraw their money. As people lost their confidence, banks failed left and right. The stock market collapsed for the first time in American history and closed. By September 24, the New York Clearing House had suspended cash payments in New York, but correspondent banks continued to supply cash to their respondent banks. However, later that day, Henry Clews & Co., the correspondent bank for John Johnston and Co., was suspended. In lieu of its suspension, the bank directed its respondent banks to send their drafts payable to alternate banking institutions. John Johnston and Co. was directed to use the firm Allen, Stephens and Co. At the time of the bank's suspension, Henry Clews announced his bank held a large amount of currency and more than $800,000 in securities with Fourth National Bank. He professed that as the crowds stormed his bank and his cash on hand was depleted, he was confident the securities at Fourth National Bank would see him through the crisis. But the bank refused to certify his checks, and by holding his bonds as security, he was forced to suspend.

In Port Huron, the panic was watched closely. On September 27, 1873, when the panic began to cause issues with a few Detroit banks, the local businessmen of the city decided to take action to avoid a panic locally. They issued a signed declaration that read:

> *We, the undersigned citizens and businessmen of Port Huron, having full confidence in the solvency of the First National Bank, the Port Huron Savings Bank, and the banking firm of John Johnston & Co., and being convinced that they are able to pay every dollar of their liabilities and*

have a good surplus and desiring in the present crisis to sustain them and prevent any movement for a withdrawal of deposits made with them, which might lead to a temporary suspension and great disarrangement of business hereby agree to pledge ourselves to deposit with them all money that can be spared from our businesses and not to draw on them except when absolutely necessary for business purposes. And we urge all persons having deposits in any of the said banks not to withdraw them, but to let their money remain there, assuring them that it is safe and that their interests, no less than those of the whole city and county, will be best served by such action.

Later that day, the local bankers of the city held a meeting at the First National Bank. Present were D.B. Harrington, Henry McMorran, Henry Howard, John E. Miller Jr., C.F. Harrington, John Johnston and O'Brien Atkinson. They resolved at the meeting to decline to pay currency during the present crisis beyond the actual necessities of business. A little later that day, rumors of John Johnston's solvency began spreading again, as the suspension of his correspondent bank, Henry Clews and Co., was called into question.

THE BEGINNING OF THE END

In April 1873, before the panic occurred, John Miller passed away. John Johnston ran for his vacant mayoral seat and was elected. Between 1872 and 1873, the city built its new water system. The total cost was $170,000, all of which the city borrowed at 10 percent interest. It was an enormous expense for the city, but John Johnston believed the cost was well worth the investment, and he publicly supported building the system. The waterworks gave the city more protection against fires and benefited the public health. It reduced the death rate in the city by almost 50 percent. The debt would carry for many years.

After the Panic of 1873, the city experienced a short period of depression until 1879. Interest rates rose. Lumbering and shipbuilding began to slow. No growth in business or population was experienced in the city. In late 1873, while Johnston was acting Mayor the annual interest on the bonds for the waterworks were coming due and the city coffers were low. In response, the city reached out to the community for funds. It needed to come up with $60,000, so it asked its citizens to help by purchasing bonds at interest to avoid its credit being damaged. Believing in the value of Port Huron and the water project, John Johnston stepped forward and purchased $40,000 in bonds. He was the only person in the community who did so. He did this despite whatever hardship he bore from the panic in September.

In 1874, Fred L. Wells retired from Johnston and Co. The company reorganized with new partners, Miron Williams, John S. Botsford and Alexander McDairmed. At the same time, the conflict over control of the city funds flared up again, but this time, it brought pioneer Henry McMorran, as acting City Treasurer, into the fight. By 1875, Johnston no longer held the mayoral seat, Nathan L. Boynton did. This caused Alderman Bancroft to propose a resolution to amend the city charter concerning the treasurer position; the amendment would require the treasurer to deposit the city funds into the bank that offered to pay the highest rate of interest. The plan called for bids to be placed each year by competing banks to determine which bank would be granted the right to hold the city funds. Bancroft and Mayor Nathan L. Boynton also ordered the city marshal to hold all city funds in his possession until after the new resolution was passed. Henry McMorran did not appreciate the new resolution and felt it deviated from the standard practice of his office as dictated by the city charter. In prior years, the city marshal turned the funds over to the treasurer after collection. In early December, the competitive banking resolution passed, but it did not take effect until January 1, 1876. This placed Treasurer Henry McMorran in a compromising position until after the new year, as the funds were supposed to be in his possession for which he was bonded. Henry McMorran did not take kindly to being placed in this position. He felt his right to carry out the duties of his public office was being dictated by members of the city council.

By mid-December, Bancroft started to spread rumors that McMorran would not comply with the new ordinance passed by the city council. Henry called the funds being held by the city marshal a manipulation on the part of Democrats of the council. He highlighted how holding these funds was costing the city valuable interest. In a letter to the council, McMorran stated:

Of all silly pretenses, that the Marshal should not be expected to pay over tax collections until a demand was made on him, is the silliest. What has he paid over anything for? Does not the warrant accompanying the tax roll into his hands contemplate, if it does not specifically command him to pay the money over to the Treasury? Must a public officer be directed to do his plain duty? But I did make repeated demands on him to turn over the city's money and he refused to do so, saying "wait until the committee meets." The fact remains that James Gain, City Marshal, has now in his hands

$12,000 to $15,000 of the city's money. It does not belong to him, but to the city, of whose funds the charter makes the Treasurer the sole custodian. He holds in violation of law thousands of dollars belonging to the city. By doing so he forces the city to pay interest on its obligations which it cannot meet or want of these funds, but which it would cancel and stop interest if the Marshal did not lawfully withhold the moneys. This cheating of the city out of the use of its money is as shameful and barefaced an outrage as any of the plundering deeds of the Tammany ring. It is defrauding the city, and the Democratic members of the council who sustain the Marshal in his action are guilty of conniving at fraud.

Bancroft combated McMorran by trying to discredit him in the press. He accused McMorran of failing to make his reports on time to the city council since assuming office. Again, McMorran wrote to the council. His letter was published in the press under the title "A Card from Treasurer McMorran." In the letter, he accused the city council of acting like "monarchs" and took the defensive:

I shall not be bribed by favor or smiles or deterred by scolding or threats. This is my position plainly stated. Mr. Bancroft seems to call in question my truthfulness, honesty, and integrity, while he would silence all questions in reference to his own by an egotistical reference to "a character for honesty, business integrity, and a residence in this city for the past thirty years." My character is quite as dear to me as Mr. Bancroft's can be to him, and when he attempts to assail it from my quarter, he will not find it without a defender. I have lived and grown up in this community from childhood and poverty, and although my assumptions may not have been so great or my airs so patronizing, I do not regard it as evidence of egotism to invite the most searching comparison for honor, business integrity, and manliness with that of Mr. Bancroft.

In late January 1876, after McMorran's fight with the city council was over and the city funds were in his possession, he gave John Johnston and Co. the contract to hold the city's money. In January 1877, the annual contract expired, and the city requested the funds be removed to another banking firm. At the time of withdrawal, Johnston was unable to pay the funds back to the city. Alderman Fitzgerald reported in February at a council meeting that John Johnston and Co. had refused to settle and pay over the moneys or bonds belonging to the city. This was the first indication John Johnston and Co. was in financial trouble. By May, John Johnston and Co. suspended. In addition to holding the city's funds, the firm was also holding $18,000 of county and state monies, which Johnston had deposited in his bank as acting County Treasurer. Johnston was ordered by the county to turn over all his personal property to satisfy all his creditors.

A meeting of his creditors was determined, and on the day of the meeting, fifty-nine people presented a total of $43,926 in claims. A committee to represent the creditors was established that included John P. Sanborn, C.G. Meisel, H.C. Hope, James Beard, John Cole and Lewis Potts. Eventually, Johnston disclosed that the Panic of 1873 and foreclosed land mortgages were the reasons his banking firm was experiencing trouble. By July, Johnston's banking partners, Miron Williams (Henry McMorran's father-in-law) and John S. Botsford, assured creditors they would each effect a loan of $20,000 to benefit the creditors. Capitalists in New York were contacted to effectuate these loans, and they were turned down. Their attorney, B.C. Farrand, sought help from lenders in Detroit, but also failed to secure the loans for Williams and Botsford.

In anticipation of bankruptcy, Miron Williams began deeding out his land to his family members to avoid losing all his property. His property

A photograph of the sketch of the John Johnston residence in Port Huron, Michigan, as illustrated in *Atlas of St. Clair County*, 1878. *Courtesy of the Isabell family collection.*

was seized by the courts. Johnston made an agreement with B.C. Farrand and James Beard to give over his individual property to benefit his creditors. Because Johnston, Williams and Botsford were only able to raise enough money to pay off half of their debts with $20,000 still owing, they had to declare bankruptcy.

Johnston sold all his personal property to pay back the county and city funds. Because Johnston was still shy $7,625, James Moffat, James Beard, William Bancroft and Wallace Ames helped him pay the remainder of the debt. After his bankruptcy in May 1878, John Johnston left the area. He moved to Chicago, where he remained for a few years before setting out for Colorado.

From the Johnston Mansion to the Reed House

On May 25, 1877, Johnston signed over his home by deed to B.C. Farrand and James Beard in accordance with his agreement to turn over all his personal property to satisfy his creditors. They sold the house on January 17, 1878, for $1,000 to Peter W. Reed, MD. The beautiful home was located on the corner of Wall and Sixth Streets. It is described in the deed as Lots 16 and 18 of Block 56 in White's Plat. Today, it is known as 1026 Sixth Street.

Peter W. Reed was born in 1827 near Belleville, Hastings County, Ontario, Canada. His grandparents immigrated to Canada from the Mohawk River Valley in New York before the Revolutionary War. Peter did not receive a formal education in his youth. His father died when he was young, so he worked to help provide for his family. From the age of sixteen to twenty, he served an apprenticeship and worked as a journeyman. Later, he suffered some health issues and went to work as a currier. In 1850, he married his wife, Ann. Peter began reading medical books and developed an interest in the material. He taught himself about medicine by reading and through trial and error. He was extremely interested in the Eclectic practice of medicine. This practice combined the use of physical therapy and botanical remedies in treatment. The Eclectic practice of medicine was rooted in Native American medicine, which used plants for medicinal purposes.

Peter would work to provide for his family during the day and study his medical books at night. In 1857, he moved to Terre Haute, Indiana, to set up a medical practice and work as a physician. He did not have much success. A few years later, he moved back to Canada and settled in Madoc. On his return to Canada, Peter found much debate in the medical community regarding the different schools of medicine. Being a believer in the Eclectic practice, Peter set out to circulate a petition to have the Canadian government recognize Eclectic medicine as a practice. He was successful in his endeavors, and an Eclectic Board was established in Toronto to grant licenses to practice this form of medicine.

In 1861, Peter moved to Port Huron, where he built an extensive medical practice. In the *American Biographical History*, Peter alludes to a prejudice existing in the regular medical community against medical professionals who practiced Eclectic medicine. While Peter felt his work in the profession was respected and recognized by members of the local medical community, the absence of a certified board in Michigan made it impossible for him to obtain a medical degree and the credibility of being a recognized medical professional. To obtain a medical degree, he moved to Cincinnati. In 1865, he graduated from the Eclectic Medical College of Cincinnati, Ohio. In his later years, Peter became known as one of the leading Eclectic medicine physicians in the country. He was instrumental in working to procure the passage of an act in the Michigan Legislature that recognized the practice and allowed for the organization of the State Eclectic Medical and Surgical Association in Michigan. Peter served as both Vice-President and President of this organization in his lifetime.

Peter had medical offices in Port Huron at the northeast corner of Bard and River Streets from 1871 to 1872, and on the northeast corner of Superior and Butler Streets from 1873 to 1878. In 1881, he practiced out of his house at 1026 Sixth Street. His wife, Ann, worked alongside him as a midwife. Together, the couple birthed many babies in the Port Huron area. Peter and Ann had three children of their own, Robert H. Reed, William Reed and Jane Reed. Both Robert and William worked for the Peerless Cement Company in their youth. Robert Reed married Georgianna Isabel Hall in 1888. Afterward, he went to work in North Dakota as a railroad engineer. Robert's love for his wife and family are intimately expressed in the letters he sent home. While he worked in North Dakota, his family returned to the Port Huron area. He returned to them in 1898, after the death of his father. Robert inherited his father's home at 1026 Sixth Street through his estate. At the time of Dr. Peter Reed's death, the home was no longer known as the Johnston mansion but was called the Reed House.

Robert moved into the home with his wife and six children. The Reed family was active in the First Presbyterian Church. Robert was a member of Pine Grove Lodge No. 11, F. and A.M. His children attended Port Huron schools. In a school photograph of his young daughter, Elizabeth Thacher Reed,

A photograph of the Reed House, circa 1900. *Courtesy of the Isabell family collection.*

The Robert H. Reed family, circa 1910. Elizabeth Thacher Reed can be seen on the top far left. *Courtesy of the Isabell family collection.*

she is described as having an active interest in the women's suffrage movement. According to her granddaughter, Elizabeth Isabell Wickings, Elizabeth was a very intelligent woman and suffragette. She was actively involved in the women's rights movement in the late 1910s and early 1920s.

Elizabeth Thacher Reed married George L. Isabell in 1925 in Port Huron. In 1936, their son Harvey E. Isabell was born. Harvey graduated from Port Huron High School in 1954 and went on to attend St. Clair County Community College. He enlisted in the U.S.

Elizabeth Thacher Reed, circa 1920. *Courtesy of the Isabell family collection.*

Navy and served from 1954 to 1958. He reenlisted in 1968 and served two tours in Vietnam. After the war, he continued in the service until his retirement in 1984. He was a member of the Port Huron Masonic Lodge No. 58 and the Moslem Shriners. Harvey passed away at the age of eighty-five on December 20, 2021.

The information on the Reed family and their home is only available to us through the diligent and timely research efforts of Harvey E. Isabell; the preservation efforts of his daughter, Elizabeth Isabell Wickings; and the writing on the family's history by his granddaughter, Erica Wickings. Both Erica and Elizabeth reside in the Port Huron community. Erica, at the time of this writing, is attending St. Clair County Community College in pursuit of a marketing degree. Much like her grandfather, she enjoys and appreciates research and history.

THE CHARLES A. HAMMOND AMERICAN LEGION POST 8

Today, 1026 Sixth Street is home to the Charles A. Hammond American Legion Post 8. This organization was originally chartered in 1919 and named after Lieutenant Charles A. Hammond, a native of Port Huron. Mr. Hammond honorably gave his life for his country in World War I. During my interview with the Wickings family, they explained that it is their belief a part of the original homestead structure still exists on the legion site. It has been many years since they toured the building, so they could not

The Charles A. Hammond American Legion Post 8 in Port Huron, Michigan, 2023. *Author's photograph*.

pinpoint the exact location. However, Elizabeth fondly remembers being shown the area on a tour years ago.

According to Erica Wickings,

> *This building is full of memorabilia of the different wars that its members, former members and their family members had served in; however, that is not all this building features. The American Legion Post 8 is also the home to a bar, where they also serve food to the public, this includes their very popular Fish Fry Fridays. This building holds deep meaning to Port Huron and the military families that live here, as it serves as a historical location, tying us to our past so it does not become forgotten, even as the generations that had experienced these wars pass away. It holds deep meaning to myself as well, it served as a reminder not only of my departed grandfather's service to our country, as he was a retired and disabled veteran who frequented the American Legion Post 8, but this building also serves as a reminder of my family, the Reed Family, who had come to Port Huron from Ontario and had their homestead on this exact location.*

Erica's words resonate with the connectedness and commonality associated with family and small-town living. Her words serve to remind us that life is a journey. And whether we know it or not at the time, our life experiences can leave a lasting impression on our community for others to experience and appreciate down the line.

The American Legion Post 8 also holds fond memories for me. In the 1990s, me and my friend Julie used to meet my grandmother there to play bingo periodically. Since I lived in Lexington, Michigan, at the time, these get-togethers gave me the opportunity to visit my grandmother and good friend. Julie lived in the apartments located in the old Sanborn home on the corner of Seventh and Union Streets. We would walk to her apartment after bingo. Those youthful summer night walks filled with laughter are some of my best memories of home, memories that will be a part of me for the rest of my life. While researching and writing this story, the meetings and personal exchanges I shared with Erica and Elizabeth Wickings were always a pleasure and a joy. Our shared love for our hometown, the similarities in our background and our lifestyle choices all came together effortlessly and easily. Out of our encounters, we have made a connection that will bond us for life.

Port Huron may have been built on the backs of the lumber, water transportation and railroad industries, but the relationships forged among its people and community are the ties that bind it together. This is true from a historical perspective and is prevalent today. Thank you, Erica and Elizabeth Wickings, for going on this journey with me and for trusting me with your story. Cheers to new friendships and hometown bonds!

3

TIMBER

By the 1840s, the lumbermen of New England had cut through the vast forests of Maine and New York, causing them to send out scouts and surveyors to find new pinelands. They found the forests of Michigan to be full of their desired product. Thus, lumber became one of the earliest industries in the State of Michigan. Two native residents of Maine and New Hampshire, Cummings Sanborn and James W. Sanborn, came to the Port Huron area and worked in the lumber trade during its infancy. These pioneers did more than just build sawmills, cut timber and run logs to make their living. In fact, they slowly became experts in surveying, scouting, real estate, log booming, milling, shipping and the mercantile business.

As the pine logs were cut in the forest, they were transported to sawmills via Michigan's many lakes and streams by numerous lumber operators. Sorting the logs when they reached their destination proved to be confusing. Log marks were used to designate log owners. However, the marks were simple and limited in design in the early lumber days, causing issues between lumber operators. Lumbermen were not the only ones questioning the transport of lumber. Landowners that bordered the lakes and streams also questioned the lumber operators' use of the lakes and streams for transportation purposes.

Two early legal cases relevant to the industry came out of St. Clair County, *Moore v. Sanborne* and *Ames v. The Port Huron Log Driving and Booming Company*. These important cases shaped the lumber industry throughout the state. Taking a closer look at these cases and the parties involved offers us the opportunity to expand our knowledge of these men and the industry that dominated St. Clair County from 1850 to 1870.

THE MEN INVOLVED IN THE *MOORE V. SANBORNE* CASE

Cummings Sanborn

Cummings Sanborn was born on January 15, 1799, in North Haverhill, New Hampshire. In his early years, Cummings showed signs of being a scholar, leading him to become a teacher by profession. As a young man, he taught school in Staten Island and the surrounding area. In 1833, he decided to move to Michigan. He continued to teach, saving his earnings in the hopes of entering the lumber industry. In 1834, he purchased land in Section 27 in the vicinity of Smiths Creek and Scott Road in present-day Kimball Township, Michigan. He constructed a water sawmill on this land along the Pine River and operated a store out of Marysville. A few years later, he moved to Port Huron.

While living in Port Huron, Cummings went into the mercantile business with his nephew Martin Gillett and his brothers-in-law, Allen and Henry Fish, on the corner of Military and Water Streets. He continued to cut and log timber on his Kimball Township property, and he built a steam mill in partnership with John Howard and John Beebe on the north side of Griswold Street. Cummings also invested in shipbuilding to ship his lumber. He owned the schooners *Hard Times* and *M. Kingman*. Before Edmund Fitzgerald became a famous shipbuilder in Port Huron, he served as the master of Cummings's vessels.

James W. Sanborn and Charles Merrill

Abner Coburn was born in 1803 in Canaan, Somerset County, Maine. His father, Eleszar Coburn, was a surveyor. Abner learned to conduct surveys in his youth, which gave him an extensive knowledge of timberlands. In 1830, he went into the lumber business with his father and brother. They

Left: A sketch portrait of Cummings Sanborn, as illustrated in *Genealogy of the Family of Samborne or Sanborn in England and America, 1194–1898. Courtesy of Family Search.*

Right: A sketch portrait of James W. Sanborn, as illustrated in *Genealogy of the Family of Samborne or Sanborn in England and America, 1194–1898. Courtesy of Family Search.*

constructed a sawmill on the Kennebec River in Maine under the firm name E. Coburn and Sons. They purchased large tracts of timberlands in Maine to supply their mill.

Charles Merrill was born in 1792 in Falmouth, Maine. He was the son of General James Merrill. In his youth, he lived in Portland, Maine, where he invested in a mercantile business that eventually failed. In debt, he moved for a brief time to Virginia, where he subcontracted to build a railroad in Petersburg. This allowed him to pay off his debts in Portland. After he built the railroad in Virginia, he moved back to Maine and accepted a contract to build a road from Lincoln to Houlton, Maine. These projects helped educate and expand Charles's knowledge of timberlands, which led him to begin investing in real estate. In 1835, Charles partnered with Abner Coburn and purchased twenty-five thousand acres of land in St. Clair and Sanilac Counties, which included acreage in Section 27 of Kimball Township near the Cummings Sanborn property.

With an interest in acquiring more Michigan land, Charles needed someone to oversee and manage the twenty-five thousand acres he held with Abner Coburn. So, he sent for his young nephew James W. Sanborn, who was in Falmouth, Maine, and asked him to come to Michigan to handle the job for him. In 1836, James came to Michigan and settled in Metamora,

Left: A sketch portrait of Charles Merrill, as illustrated in *The History of Detroit and Michigan*, Vol. 2, by Silas Farmer, 1889. *Courtesy of Google Books.*

Right: A sketch portrait of Stephen Moore, as illustrated in *The History of Detroit and Michigan*, Vol. 2, by Silas Farmer, 1889. *Courtesy of Google Books.*

Lapeer County, and began overseeing the investment. By 1845, James W. Sanborn had gained extensive knowledge of the lumber and real estate business managing the Merrill and Coburn lands. With his new knowledge and some money in his pocket, James went into the business with his brother-in-law, Alvah Sweetser. Together, they purchased large tracts of pineland on the Saginaw and Muskegon Rivers and their tributaries, the Au Sable and Pine Rivers on Thunder Bay, and in the Upper Peninsula. James and Alvah moved to Port Huron in 1847. James continued to oversee his uncle's lands in Michigan until 1848, after which time Charles moved to Detroit and began overseeing the lands himself.

Charles became one of the wealthiest lumberers in the State of Michigan. He built the Merrill Block in Detroit in 1858. By 1863, he was in partnership with Thomas W. Palmer, the son of Thomas Palmer Sr. and Mary Witherell. Thomas married Charles Merrill's only daughter, Lizzie Pitts Merrill. Charles Merrill's earnings in 1865 amounted to $52,307, which today would total just under $1 million. Thomas Palmer became a rich man himself. In 1897, the Palmers donated 140 acres of land Thomas had inherited from his grandfather, the Michigan Territorial Judge James Witherell, which became the famous Palmer Park in Detroit.

Franklin, Reuben and Stephen Moore

In 1837, Franklin and Reuben Moore purchased property in Section 7 in Kimball Township in the vicinity of Sparling and Griswold Roads, about nine miles northwest of Cummings Sanborn. Franklin and Reuben were brothers who were born in Manchester, New Hampshire. Their father, Joseph Moore, operated a lumber mill on the Merrimack River in New Hampshire where the boys learned the trade. The two brothers came to Michigan on a lumber prospecting tour in 1832. Recognizing the value of the timberland, they decided to stay.

They lived in Detroit for a time, where Franklin operated a dry goods business with his brother-in-law, Zachariah Chandler, under the firm name Moore and Chandler. Zachariah Chandler and Franklin Moore became wealthy businessmen in Detroit. Later in his life, Chandler entered the political arena, becoming one of the most influential politicians in Michigan and Washington between 1848 and 1879. Chandler started his career in public service as the mayor of Detroit, after which he became a staunch abolitionist who supported the Underground Railroad. He went on to become one of the founding members of the National Republican Party. He became actively involved in matters related to the Civil War as a member of Congress, in which he served four terms as a Michigan senator. From the Senate, he went on to become Secretary of the Interior under the Grant administration, and in his later years, he served as the Chair of the Republican National Committee.

Reuben Moore eventually settled in St. Clair, Michigan, and went into the lumber manufacturing business with his other brother, Stephen. Together, they purchased pinelands to feed their lumber business. The Moore brothers continued in business together until 1863. In 1867, Stephen and Franklin Moore went into the lumber business with Russell A. Algier. The business was known as Moore Algier and Company. They constructed their own sawmill at the foot of Eighteenth Street in Detroit and eventually operated a second mill out of Bay City, Michigan. They continued in this business enterprise together until Franklin's death in 1877.

Moore v. Sanborne, pleading caption.
Courtesy of the Michigan Archives.

NAVIGATIONAL WATER

Cummings Sanborn, James W. Sanborn, Alvah Sweetser, Charles Merrill, and the Moore brothers were actively engaged in cutting timber on their properties in Kimball Township. They would cut the timber and throw it into the Pine River, where it would float out to the mouth of the St. Clair River. From there, it would be floated to Port Huron or Detroit. In the spring of 1850, Reuben Moore hired a man by the name of Stewart to cut the timber on his property in Section 7 and float it to the mouth of the St. Clair River. His timber got mixed in with the timber being floated by James W. Sanborn, Alvah Sweetser, Charles Merrill and Cummings Sanborn. The logs jammed on the Pine River on the properties owned by Cummings and James Sanborn, which caused all the logs to mix together. Cummings bore the expense of removing the jam and floating the logs to the St. Clair River. Having an interest in the matter, James Sanborn, Alvah Sweetser and Charles Merrill brought a nuisance suit against Reuben Moore to recoup the expenses.

The case was heard by Judge Joseph T. Copeland in the summer of 1850 in the Circuit Court of St. Clair County. Just before the case was brought forward, Michigan's legislature passed a new Constitution, which abolished the old county court system and established the state into six circuit court districts. It also called for judges in the circuits to be elected instead of appointed. St. Clair County became part of the circuit composed of Oakland, Macomb, St. Clair and Sanilac Counties, known as the Sixth Circuit. The elected judges of each circuit also formed the Michigan Supreme Court. Judge Copeland, who had acted alongside Judge Bunce under the old county court system, was elected the new circuit judge for St. Clair County. At the time of his election, Judge Copeland resided in Pontiac, so the trial was heard there. The case presented a unique situation for lumbermen to finally settle the navigable waters question in Michigan.

At trial, arguments from both sides focused on dividing the Pine River into two parts, establishing the place of division at the "Deer Licks." It was argued that the route along the stream above the Deer Licks was a navigable waterway during a period of only two to three weeks a year. Whereas the route along the stream below the Deer Licks was navigable at any time of the year. Moore's defense hinged on the English Common Law standard for navigable waters. His attorney argued that for a waterway to be navigable under common law, a boat had to be able to travel along it. And since the point above the Deer Licks was navigable by boat only two or three weeks out of the year, it was not a public highway according to the English Common Law standard, thus rendering Stewart's use of the stream above the Deer Licks to float logs for Moore was illegal. And if Stewart's use of the stream was deemed illegal, Stewart, whom Moore had hired to do the work was culpable for the damage, not Moore. At the end of the trial, the jury found Moore to be responsible for the nuisance on the Sanborn property.

After the trial, Moore filed an appeal and took his argument to the Michigan Supreme Court. The case was heard and decided in 1852. In its ruling decision, the court decided the English Common Law standard for navigable waters was too narrow in scope and not applicable to the waterways of Michigan. The court held:

> *The servitude of the public interest depends rather upon the purpose for which the public requires the use of its streams, than upon any particular mode of use—and hence, in a region where the principal business is lumbering, or the pursuit of any particular branch of manufacturing or trade, the public claim to a right of passage along its streams must depend upon their capacity for the use to which they can be made subservient. Upon many of our streams, although of sufficient capacity for navigation by boats, they are never seen—whilst rafts of lumber of immense value, and mill logs which are counted by thousands, are annually floated along them to market. Accordingly, we find that a capacity to float rafts of logs in those States where the manufacture of lumber is prosecuted as a branch of trade, is recognized as a criterion of the public right of passage and of use, upon the principle already adverted to, that such right is to be ascertained from the public necessity and occasion for such use.*

Moore v. Sanborne established that a stream with a capacity for floatage was navigable and that all persons using it held equal rights. This case established the "log-float" test as the test to determine navigability of Michigan's waterways, and it remains controlling law today. According to Terra Bowling and Madeline Doten, research counsel and research associate for the National Sea Grant Law Center:

> *In 1874, the Michigan Court of Appeals adopted the recreational use test—which defines waters as navigable if they are capable of being navigated by oar or motor propelled small craft. However, the Michigan Supreme Court expressly rejected this test less than 10 years later. Thus, the log-float test, not the recreational use test, must be used to determine the*

navigability of the Michigan rivers used as water trails. There are three methods to determine whether a steam passes the log-float test. First, tests may be conducted to show that the river can actually support the floatation of logs. Second, records may be utilized to illustrate historical usage of the river to transport logs. Third, a comparison may be done between the characteristics of the river in question and other streams that have already been determined navigable.

THE PORT HURON LOG DRIVING AND BOOMING COMPANY

The *Moore v. Sanborne* decision opened Michigan's waterways and streams to lumbermen to transport their timber without interference, which expanded the industry across the state. More lumbermen putting logs in rivers and tributaries called for the regulation of running and booming logs. On January 3, 1855, Omar D. Conger, the representative from Port Huron in the Michigan Senate, called for a bill to "regulate the floating of rafts, logs, and lumber upon navigable streams within the state." According to the record of proceedings contained in the *Journal of the Senate of the State of Michigan*, Conger revised the bill on January 20, 1855, and presented it to the senate as "An Act to provide for the formation of companies for running, driving, booming and rafting logs, timber, and lumber and for regulating the floatage thereof."

The lumbermen in St. Clair County wasted no time forming a company under Conger's new law. On March 1, 1855, the Port Huron Log Driving and Booming Company was incorporated by lumbermen from Port Huron, Detroit, Brockway, Lexington, Lynn and Newport (present-day Marine City). The members of the company were (1) John Wells, (2) Alvah Sweetser, (3) F.H. Vandenburgh, (4) W.B. and J. Hibbard, (5) William Sanborn, (6) Fred Wells, (7) Christ Reese, (8) N. Roberts, (9) Allen and Henry Fish, (10) James W. Sanborn, (11) Lewis Brockway, (12) John P. Sanborn, (13) George W. Pack, (14) E.R. Budd, (15) Charles Duker, (16) Baughman Hubbard King, (17) Willard Parker, (18) Frederick F. White, (19) C. Hadley, (20) William Allison, (21) T.L. Davis, (22) Aloney and David Rust, (23) M.F. Bailey, (24) Dudley Wheeler and (25) Eugene Smith.

A Brief Sketch of Some of the Lumbermen

In 1854, John Wells and his son Fred built a mill on the south side of the Black River for the purpose of sawing timber from the lands they owned in Sanilac County. They ran this mill until 1880. Allen and Henry Fish partnered in business for many years with Cummings Sanborn. After Sanborn's death in 1852, they went into the milling business with Simon Petit and erected a mill on the St. Clair River. Petit was accidently killed three years later. The Fish brothers continued the operation of the mill they had owned with Petit until 1858, when they built a new mill in Kimball Township, south of the Port Huron and Lapeer Plank Road. The Fish brothers owned the plank road in partnership with James W. Sanborn, Lewis Brockway and John Beard. After the lumber interests in St. Clair County began to dry up, the Fish brothers purchased the controlling interest in the road and used it to haul lumber from their mill.

Christ Reese and Ralph Wadhams were partners who operated a mercantile business in Detroit in 1823. In 1830, Ralph left the business and built a mill on the Black River in Wadhams. In 1845, William Sanborn and his brother, John P. Sanborn, came to the Port Huron area to work with their uncle James W. Sanborn. In Michigan, William Sanborn learned the art of timber scouting and surveying work under his uncle in the public land office. After the Civil War, William operated a sawmill on the St. Clair River in Marysville, Michigan, where he sawed the pine timber he cut from his properties in Iosco, Alcona and Oscoda Counties. He sold the property to Nelson and Barney Mills in 1871. This mill was located on the old Morton Salt property north of Bunce Road in Marysville.

From 1842 to 1858, Aloney and David Rust operated a mill in partnership with their shipbuilding uncle, Sam Ward, in Marine City. The mill would alternate between cutting lumber for Sam's shipbuilding business and cutting logs for local lumbermen. In addition to operating the mill in Marine City, both Aloney and David Rust often went on scouting expeditions in the Upper Peninsula with their cousin David Ward. David was also a nephew of Sam Ward. David was a highly sought-after timberland scout for wealthy lumbermen. Charles Merrill often employed his services.

David's fee for his scouting services consisted of a one-fourth interest of any lands purchased by his clients. He considered these lands an investment for his future. In 1857, when David was thirty-four years old, he felt worn out from having lived for extended periods in the wilderness under extreme conditions while scouting. He felt it was time to pin his hopes on the lumber

A log mark used by James W. Sanborn. *Courtesy of Michigan State University.*

industry to gain independent wealth. At the time, his good friend Omar
D. Conger advised him not to enslave himself to the lumbering industry.
Conger stressed the physical and mental hardship David had endured over
his many years of scouting and advised him to sell his pineland, build a house
and settle down for the rest of his days. David did not heed Conger's advice.
He began lumbering the land he had acquired as a scout and invested in
the Tittabawassee Boom Company in the 1860s. Eventually, David's efforts

paid off. He got rich from cutting, booming and selling the timber on his lands. David Ward lived for a brief time in Marine City, Port Huron, Gratiot County and Saginaw until he settled for good with his family on a nice farm at Orchard Lake in Oakland County.

Being acquainted in the lumber business for years, James W. Sanborn, Aloney Rust and David Rust partnered as Sanborn, Rust and Co. in the 1860s on the west side of the state. There, they managed an extensive timber operation on the Muskegon River in Big Rapids, Michigan. James W. Sanborn and the Rust brothers had come to the state during the infancy of the lumber trade, and by the 1850s, they had purchased timberlands in Mecosta, Sanilac, Otsego, Cheboygan, Presque Isle, Montmorency, Osceola, Mackinac, Missaukee, Alger, Schoolcraft, Montcalm, Huron and Gratiot Counties. In business together, they ran and boomed their logs from their various property holdings via the Muskegon, Au Sable and Tittabawasee Rivers. Their firm was so big and so well known among the lumbering community, in 1874, Stephen Moore went to work on the Muskegon River for Sanborn, Rust and Co. as their superintendent despite being in the lumber business with his brother, Franklin, and Russell A. Algier. Even though Sanborn died in 1870, his businesses were kept intact, and his interests were managed by the trustee of his estate, J.P. Sanborn. Outside of the Sanborn, Rust and Co. firm, the Rust brothers also ran a mill in Saginaw they operated under the firm name Rust, King and Co., to which Thomas A. Alverson worked as a foreman before he moved to Port Huron in 1874 and became a shipbuilder in the firm Dunford and Alverson. In addition to his other lumbering interests, James W. Sanborn had a business partnership with his brother-in-law, Alvah Sweetser. They operated a mill together in Worth Township in Sanilac County. He and Alvah also operated a real estate and mercantile business out of the Merchant Exchange Block in Port Huron and held ownership of the building with Martin Gillett.

AMES V. THE PORT HURON LOG DRIVING AND BOOMING COMPANY

To incorporate under the 1855 statute, the members of the Port Huron Log Driving and Booming Company were required to give their community notice of their company's name, its officers and members, its location of business, and the location of the streams or waterways the company intended to use in its course of business. The company had to file its articles of association with attached affidavits with the Michigan secretary of state. The company was also required, in its course of business, to keep a posting in its office that recorded the names of all its members, any person it did work for and its log mark(s).

In early August 1855, a log jam occurred on the Black River, while the Port Huron Log Driving and Booming Company and the Black River Steam Mill Company were both running and floating logs in it. The mill did not use the booming company's services to float its logs. Instead, it employed contracted "jobbers" to handle the running and booming for them. After the logs became jammed and intermixed, the Port Huron Log Driving and Booming Company took control of the run and expended its time and efforts driving all the intermixed logs. It placed the 135 logs belonging to the Black River Steam Mill in its boom. It also made note of the number of logs it ran for the mill after the jam occurred. According to the new law, when a log jam occurred and caused the intermixing of logs, the company that handled the problem was allowed to sell any logs it handled through public sale. This sale was intended to allow the company to recoup the additional expenses incurred in handling the log jam.

To sell the Black River Steam Mill's 135 logs via public sale, the Port Huron Log Driving and Booming Company was required to post a notice of the sale and identify what logs it was selling. The Black River Steam Mill immediately objected to the sale of their logs and accused the booming company of illegally removing the 135 logs from its boom. The booming company ignored the mill's objection, and the auction took place on August 24, 1855. At the sale, the booming company purchased the logs for half the price of their retail value. This caused three separate cases to be filed and brought before the court. The first suit was brought by the Black River Steam Mill Company against Frederick White, the acting secretary of the Port Huron Log Driving and Booming Company. In retaliation, the Port Huron Log Driving and Booming Company filed a second suit against the Black River Steam Mill to recoup additional expenses it incurred during the jam not covered by the sale of the logs. The third suit was filed by Tilden Ames and Alanson Sheeley against the Port Huron Log Driving and Booming Company for the 135 logs that had been sold at public auction. Ames and Sheeley became involved because they had prepaid the Black River Steam Mill for this exact number of logs. They were told by the mill their logs were now part of a lawsuit. Expecting to receive what they had paid for, they also filed suit.

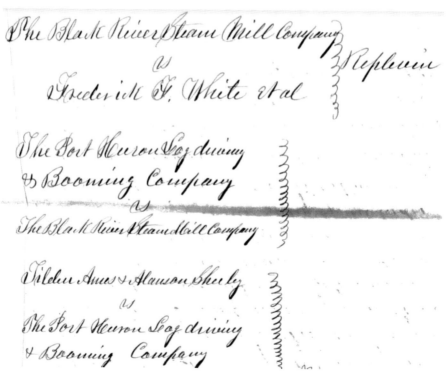

Nº of Logs	Marks	measurement
28	X	12738 feet
60	S I	19511 — u
16	S1	6806 u
6	O.W.	2268 u
3	II	932 u
16	I	1093 u
1	I	304 u

Log marks used by the Black River Steam Mill, as illustrated in the *Ames v. The Port Huron Log Driving & Booming Company* case file. *Courtesy of the Michigan Archives.*

The Black River Steam Mill Company

v.

Frederick F. White et al

} Replevin

The Port Huron Log driving
& Booming Company

v.

The Black River Steam Mill Company

Tilden Ames & Alanson Sheely

v.

The Port Huron Log driving
& Booming Company

The pleading caption for the three cases combined into the *Ames v. The Port Huron Log Driving & Booming Company. Courtesy of the Michigan Archives.*

Since all three of these matters involved the same logs, Judge Copeland of the circuit court caused the various parties to consolidate their cases into one under the caption, *Tilden Ames vs. the Port Huron Log Driving and Booming Company*. Ames and Sheeley employed John S. Collins as counsel, and the Port Huron Log Driving and Booming Company employed the firm of Congers and Harris.

It must be noted that this case was litigated and tried between 1855 and 1863. At this time, Omar D. Conger, who represented the Port Huron Log Driving and Booming Company in this suit, was also serving as an elected member of the Michigan Senate from the Port Huron District. In addition, the statute at issue in the case was one he had worked on and introduced into legislation. Being apprised of this information, one might assume his representation of the company would present a conflict of interest. However, under the 1850 Michigan Constitution under Article IV, Section 18, a conflict of interest would only be present in instances of a state civil appointment or in a situation that involved a state or county contract. Since this case did not involve a state or country contract, Conger's representation did not present a conflict.

At the time of the trial, counsel for Ames and Sheeley argued the company was operating unlawfully as an entity, having failed to file the required affidavits with its articles of association. They also argued the booming company acted illegally by taking the logs out of the Black River Steam Mill's boom after the company had placed them there. Judge Copeland heard the arguments and found the missing affidavits to be immaterial and stated the articles themselves constituted the validity of the company. He also found that the booming company's claim on the logs had not been lost because they had initially been placed in the Black River Steam Mill's boom after the run. Copeland was not able to officially render his decision the day of the hearing because there was still a dispute over the exact dollar amount of recoverable damages existing amongst the parties. He set the case aside and asked all of the parties to come back to court in the fall term to present a stipulated dollar amount of damages and costs to the court.

When the parties came back in the fall of 1857, Judge Copeland was no longer serving as judge of the circuit court. He had resigned due to illness and to pursue an interest he had in a lumber enterprise in Saginaw, so the case was heard by his replacement, Judge Sanford M. Green. Judge Green reviewed the case and found his opinion to be in line with Judge Copeland's prior opinion. He found in favor of the booming company and

Portrait of Cummings Sanborn. *Image courtesy of the Port Huron Museum.*

awarded them $205 in damages. Unhappy with the verdict, Ames, Sheeley and the Black River Steam Mill took the case to the Michigan Supreme Court in January 1859. The supreme court reversed Judge Green's decision and granted the plaintiffs a new trial.

The second trial took place before Judge Green in February 1860. Again, Judge Green found in favor of the booming company. The Plaintiffs hired attorney William Mitchell to take the case for a second time to the Michigan Supreme Court. In its January 1863 decision, the court held the statute, which created and regulated booming companies, unconstitutional and void. The court found the law, as written, gave booming companies too much control and authorization over the floating of logs on public waters. The court also did not like the fact that the Port Huron Log Driving and Booming Company made purchase of the same logs it put up for sale at public auction. This action they also found unconstitutional. The Ames decision forced Michigan's legislature to rewrite the law. In 1864, the new law was presented and adopted as the Act to Authorize the Formation of Corporations for the Running, Booming and Rafting of Logs.

Despite its early legal troubles, the Port Huron Log Driving and Booming Company managed to stay in business for the next twenty-five years. Daniel B. Runnels said in 1896 that when he moved to Port Huron as a young man, his first job was working for Sanborn and Sweetser in the lumber industry until he took a job managing the Port Huron Log Driving and Booming Company. He recalled many disagreements between log owners floating in the Black River, which eventually caused him to develop a complete system for the rapid running of logs on the river. Ironically, after Mr. Runnels left the lumber business, he went into the steamboat business with Captain Moffat. Together, they built the infamous passenger boat *Omar D. Conger*.

A LUMBERMAN'S LEGACY

Cummings Sanborn proved to be more than just a lumberman working in the industry for profit. He also cared greatly about education and contributing to his community. His generosity to Port Huron is forever memorialized by a provision in his will, which reads, "To the common school library of the township, I give the sum of five hundred dollars and in case of the death of my son, Herbert Sanborn, without lawful issue, the additional sum of five hundred dollars." This legacy would have a value today of approximately $19,000. His generosity was acknowledged in 1904, when the new public library was opened in Port Huron. The library was built for the city using a $45,000 donation from Andrew Carnegie. Out of the 1,689 public libraries Andrew Carnegie built throughout the United States, only 750 are still functioning as libraries today.

At the new library's opening, Cummings's son Herbert Sanborn was present, along with local historian William Lee Jenks and Judge William Mitchell, the man who had won the Ames case in the Michigan Supreme Court in the 1860s. At the event, Herbert presented the library trustees with a "handsome oil painting" of his father and mother, Cummings Sanborn and Charlotte Fish Sanborn. Having been acquainted with Cummings, Judge Mitchell delivered a short speech:

> *Mr. Sanborn was a native of New Hampshire and came to the little hamlet called Black River sometime in 1840. The country around what is now Port Huron was covered with unbounded forests, traveled only by Indian trails and an occasional lumber road. Mr. Sanborn established himself in trade and soon became the owner of much property. He married Miss Charlotte Fish, a sister of Allen and Henry Fish and of Mrs. Spalding, mother of Edgar G. Spalding and Mrs. I.D. Carleton. In 1850, he called me to his house on Military Street and made his will. Among his bequests was one to the common school library of the township of Port Huron in the sum of $500.00 and provided that in case of the death of his son, Herbert C. Sanborn, without lawful issue, that an additional sum of $500.00 should be given to the library. Mr. Sanborn took up his residence in New Hampshire, where he died. There was some litigation over the settlement of his estate and the $500.00 was not paid until the son became of age and took charge of the property. In the meantime, the city had been incorporated and the town of Fort Gratiot set off from the town of Port Huron and each became entitled*

to its share of the donation. On March 23, 1872, $375.00 was paid to Port Huron, $67.49 to Port Huron Township and $57.51 to Fort Gratiot Township.

Judge Mitchell went on to express Herbert Sanborn's desire to have his father's name and memory perpetuated in the new public library in honor of his father's bequest to the old common school library. Everyone who attended the ceremony agreed that the paintings should hang on the walls inside the new building. Today, the old Carnegie library houses the Port Huron Museum, and both portraits are still hung there. We are lucky to have these special relics of our past. Without the museum and their staff of people who make it their life's work to preserve our history, our past would be lost to us. A very special thanks goes out to them for their hard work and dedication and the valuable services they provide to our community.

THE RADICAL REPUBLICANS

*O*mar Dwight Conger is one of the most highly recognized pioneers of St. Clair County. He lived in Port Huron from 1848 to 1869, when he was elected to the U.S. House of Representatives. While in Port Huron, he worked as an attorney, served as a member of the Michigan Senate (1855–59) and was known as a Radical Republican. He was present at the first Republican Party Convention, which was held in Jackson, Michigan, during the summer of 1854. Conger strongly supported the abolitionist movement and defended his belief that all men are created equal, openly defending the rights of Native and African Americans. He served five terms in Congress: four in the U.S. House of Representatives and one in the U.S. Senate.

THE CONNECTICUT WESTERN RESERVE

Omar Dwight Conger was born on April 1, 1818, in Hartwick, Otsego County, New York, to Enoch Conger and Ester West Conger. His father, being a minister, was placed in charge of several churches in the Western Reserve of Ohio when Omar was a young boy. As a result, in 1824, the family migrated from New York to Strong Ridge, Ohio, located about twelve miles from Sandusky. The area of the Western Reserve in Ohio was originally called the Connecticut Western Reserve, because it was possessed by the

WOODCUT OF WESTERN RESERVE COLLEGE, TAKEN ABOUT 1860

A woodcut of the Western Reserve College, circa 1860. *Courtesy of the Hudson Library and Historical Society.*

Colony of Connecticut under a charter from King Charles II. After the Revolutionary War, the colony ceded most of its northeastern region to the United States before the Northwest Territory was established. This section of land surrounding the southern shore of Lake Erie today encompasses the following Ohio counties: Ashtabula, Cuyahoga, Erie and Huron, Geauga, Lake, Lorain, Medina, Portage and Trumbull and some portions of Ashland, Mahoning, Ottawa, Summit and Wayne.

As a young man, Omar attended primary school at the Huron Institute at Milan, Ohio. One of his classmates at the time was Jay Cooke, who would go on to become a famous investment banker. His bank, Jay Cooke and Co., was one of the first to go bankrupt during the Panic of 1873. After graduating from the Huron Institute around 1840, Omar pursued his secondary education at Western Reserve College in Hudson, Ohio. The college relocated from Hudson to Cleveland in 1882, and today, it is known as Case Western Reserve College.

The Western Reserve and the Abolitionist Movement

At the time Omar Conger attended college, the abolitionist movement in the North began slowly gaining traction. In 1820, the Missouri Compromise essentially split the country in half from the East Coast to the Pacific Ocean, creating an imaginary border line between free states in the North and slave states in the South. When new states entered the Union, those located north of the line were deemed free states, while those that were south of the line became slave states. By the 1830s, some of the men living in northern states began to openly oppose slavery, and the area of the Western Reserve in Ohio was the most antislavery region in the country. The city of Hudson served as its hotseat. In the 1830s, abolitionist Theodore Dwight Weld visited Western Reserve College and recruited faculty members to the antislavery cause. He organized the first abolitionist society in the Western Reserve, causing an uproar among the citizens living in the area.

Contributing to the antislavery sentiment in Hudson were the passionate abolitionists Owen Brown and his son John Brown. In 1837, John committed his life to the antislavery cause after hearing about the death of Elijah Lovejoy. Elijah was a Presbyterian minister who lived in Missouri in 1827. After the 1820 Missouri Compromise, Missouri became a slave state. Elijah was strongly opposed to slavery and founded the *St. Louis Observer* newspaper. He voiced and published his opinions, often criticizing slavery and the powerful interests in the South that protected the practice. His life was often threatened, so he chose to move across the river to Alton, Illinois, where his views on slavery were more accepted.

Elijah persisted with publishing his viewpoints on slavery, resulting in continued threats to his life. An angry proslavery mob attacked the warehouse where he kept his printing press and abolitionist materials on November 7, 1837, and Elijah was fatally shot. The murder sent shockwaves across the country. At the time of Elijah's murder, John Brown was quoted as saying, "Here, before God, in the presence of these witnesses, from this time, I consecrate my life to the destruction of slavery."

John's father, Owen Brown, was so opposed to slavery and so passionate about its eradication that he split up the only church in Hudson, Ohio, over the issue. In 1842, he started his own church called the Free Congregational Church, whose members were required to swear an oath against slavery to worship there. Owen, John and other antislavery residents in Hudson

Left: John Brown, circa 1859. *Courtesy of the Library of Congress.*

Below: A proslavery mob burning down the building that housed the newspaper of abolitionist Elijah Parish Lovejoy (1802–1837) on November 7, 1837. *Courtesy of the Everett Collection/ Shutterstock.com.*

The Mob attacking the Warehouse of Godfroy Gilman & Co. Alton Ill. on the Night of the 7th Nov. 1837.

organized a branch of the Underground Railroad and helped many enslaved people escape to Canada via Lake Erie. John Brown moved from Hudson and returned with his growing family many times between 1820 and 1840.

Attending college in this atmosphere had to shape Omar's future support of the abolitionist cause. At Western Reserve College, Omar fell in love with Stella Humphrey, and they became engaged. Stella, who was born in Hudson, was the daughter of Judge Van Rensselaer Humphrey. Judge Humphrey was a cousin of John Brown, yet he later became known as a Copperhead, and he was openly opposed to the actions of his abolitionist family members. It is written that Omar and Stella broke off their engagement due to a lover's quarrel stemming from her flirtatious behavior. Is it possible the engagement was broken due to the proslavery opinions of Stella's father?

COPPER HARBOR, MICHIGAN

In 1842, after Omar graduated from Western Reserve College, he went to study law under Daniel R. Tilden in Ravenna, Ohio. Daniel R. Tilden, at the time, was partnered with Rufus P. Spalding under the firm Spalding and Tilden. A year after Omar went to work for the firm, Tilden was elected to the U.S. House of Representatives. It is written that Omar Conger went to visit his family sometime in 1845 in Plymouth, Ohio, and on his visit, he joined the geological survey team of Dr. Douglas Houghton in Michigan. In 1845, Dr. Houghton received federal funding to conduct a survey of the region after the U.S. government built Fort Wilkins and established a mineral land agency office at Copper Harbor, Michigan. Since Conger's boss, Daniel Tilden, was a U.S. representative at the time of Omar's family visit, it is likely he learned about the Houghton opportunity in Copper Harbor, Michigan, from him.

In May 1845, Conger was noted as working for Dr. Houghton at his stationary camp at Copper Harbor in the remembrances of George W. Thayer, the nephew of Lucius Lyon. Thayer had also been offered a position on the Houghton team in 1845 but had missed leaving with them from Detroit. His uncle, who had business in Montreal, offered to take young George to Copper Harbor on his way to Montreal. At the time, Lyon had recently closed his term in Congress and was appointed by

President Polk as Surveyor General of Northwest Ohio, serving Michigan, Indiana and Ohio. Speaking of his journey to join Dr. Houghton's party, Thayer noted, "Our destination was then Copper Harbor, situated about five miles from the end of Keweenaw Point, where was Fort Wilkins and two companies of United States troops. At that time, Copper Harbor was probably the most noted place on Lake Superior above the Soo." On reaching Copper Harbor, Thayer recalled,

> *At Cooper Harbor was the depot of supplies and the stationary camp of Dr. Houghton and in charge was Omar Conger, in after years, much to my surprise, a United States Senator from Michigan, who dealt out supplies to Dr. Houghton's different parties, and also took at 6 and 9 pm registrations of both barometer and thermometer. Dr. Houghton himself was there. His party, that I was to have joined in Detroit was full. The only place for me was one to be made by taking away an Indian from the doctor's brother, Jake, a slim young man about my age, who was going over the newly surveyed lines taking notes of the readings of a barometer and a thermometer at every stream, at the foot and top of every hill of any importance that the line of survey crossed.*

Because there was no room for Thayer on the Houghton team, he traveled from Copper Harbor to Mackinac, and from there, he took a boat home to Detroit. On his return to Detroit, he learned that Dr. Houghton had died in Lake Superior. Reflecting on that moment in time, Thayer stated, "In a few days a boat came from Mackinac with a report of Dr. Houghton's drowning off Eagle River in a big snowstorm on the night of the 13th of October 1845. In a minute his earthly career was closed in a terrific storm, and his boat dashed to pieces on the rocks of the forbidding coast of Keweenaw Point."

SAULT STE. MARIE, MICHIGAN

After Dr. Houghton's death, the survey was discontinued. By July 1846, Conger was in Sault Ste. Marie working in connection with a surveying party on the lakes. During his time in Sault Ste. Marie, Conger was present at the crime scene after the murder of James Schoolcraft on July 5, 1846, and is credited with drawing a diagram of the scene. James was the brother

A sketch portrait of Henry Rowe Schoolcraft, circa 1850, as illustrated in *Popular Science Monthly* 37 (May–October 1890). *Courtesy of the Library of Congress.*

of Henry R. Schoolcraft, who oversaw Michigan's Indian Department. According to Judge Joseph H. Steere,

> [James] *was walking from his residence down a path towards a field he had been clearing nearby. Bushes fringed the way and the assassin fired from an ambush at close range, inflicting upon his victim a mortal wound in the side, close below the shoulder. An ounce ball and three buckshot passed nearly through his body. Schoolcraft was a strong, athletic man in the prime of his life. He made one great leap forward and fell dead on his face. So violent was his last dying spring, made on receiving the unexpected shot, that a pair of light slippers which he wore were cleared from his feet and left sitting side by side where he stood when the shot was fired. No one witnessed the deed, but the gun had been heard and the body was shortly after discovered.*

At the time of James's death, a bitter feud over a woman existed between him and a Lieutenant Bryant Tilden. Lieutenant Tilden was then serving at Fort Brady. In his assessment of the murder, Judge Steere stated that the buck and ball cartridges used to kill Schoolcraft were likely fired from an army musket and closely resembled those cartridges issued by the government. However, instead of focusing on Tilden, suspicion was placed on local outcast John Tanner, known as the "white Indian," who had once worked as an interpreter in the Indian Department and was dismissed by Henry R. Schoolcraft in 1830.

Congers Copper and the Baltimore Mining Company

In 1846, while Conger was working in Sault Ste. Marie, he and his uncle, Jonas H. Titus, formed a copper mining company with some other men called the Baltimore Mining Company. They purchased lease numbers 267 and 269 from the Federal Mineral Land Agency. Lacking the funds to start any development on the leases, Jonas went to New York to find some prospective investors. In New York, he found a man by the name of William Hickok who was interested in becoming an investor and introduced Titus to new investors. In November 1846, Titus met with Hickok and proposed reorganizing and using the stock in the Baltimore Mining Company as collateral for the New York investors. Hickok counterproposed creating a new company that could take over the leases of the Baltimore Mining Company. He suggested the company be named the Vulcan Mining Company, holding four thousand shares of stock at $150 each, with one thousand shares being unassignable. Titus liked Hickok's idea. So, the remaining three thousand shares of stock were subscribed to by the New York investors. The total sale of the three thousand shares brought in $450,000. During Titus's visit, Hickok agreed to assign eight hundred shares of the unassignable stock to the Baltimore Mining Company in exchange for the 267 and 269 numbered leases. Jonas was paid $4,500 on the spot for the leases and left New York with the money in his pocket.

In November, when the investors met to organize the Vulcan Mining Company, the deal made between Hickok and Titus was discussed. During the meeting, the stockholders agreed to add the language "or any other lands in said mineral district that may be leased, located, or bought by

Vulcan Mining Company" to their articles. This additional language would cause litigation between the Baltimore Mining Company and the Vulcan Mining Company, as it was not part of the original agreement between Hickok and Titus.

The subscribers were worried that by issuing eight hundred shares of stock to Titus and his Baltimore Mining Company, this action might allow them to share in the profits without cost of any future mining expeditions the Vulcan Mining Company became involved in. Quietly, Hickok began buying up as much of the Baltimore Mining Company stock as he could, knowing it would be exchanged for inaccessible Vulcan shares. Hickok also hired Sam Knapp to act as the mineral agent for the Vulcan Mining Company in Detroit. He encouraged Sam to find new copper mining leases in the Upper Peninsula and to examine the 267 and 269 leases for minerals.

Sam Knapp did not find copper in the 267 and 269 leases. In July 1847, he was informed that lease number 98 was up for sale by the Ontonagon Company. He met with George C. Bates in Detroit about acquiring the lease for the Vulcan Mining Company. In September 1847, Knapp went to New York and shared his findings with the shareholders. They strongly opposed the purchase of lease number 98 on the grounds that they did not want the shareholders of the Baltimore Mining Company to have an interest in the new venture.

Hickok told Knapp to pursue lease number 98 anyway and instructed him to make the purchase under the name Hickok and Co. Back in Detroit, Knapp consulted with Conger, and he told him the Vulcan Mining Company was looking to purchase the new lease and assign it to William Hickok in trust for the Vulcan company. Conger was not happy with this arrangement and objected to it. At trial, in his deposition testimony before the Michigan Supreme Court, Knapp stated, "There was some considerable contention between Conger and me—some disagreement on this point about the papers. Conger used some pretty sharp words. I do not remember whether or not he threatened to break up the contract, but I had some fears."

Knapp went on to purchase the lease in Hickok's name and worked the lease under the Vulcan name. The lease proved fruitful. In June 1848, the shareholders met and decided to create a new company called the Minnesota Mining Company of New York. This new company was created to exclude the Baltimore Mining Company from any profits from the lease. Conger and Titus sued and lost on their appeal to the Michigan Supreme Court. This ended Conger's attempt at copper mining.

UNDER THE OAKS

By 1847, Jonas Titus was operating a water steam mill in Burtchville Township, Michigan, manufacturing about 800,000 logs a year. In 1848, Omar went to work for his uncle at his lumber mill. In 1850, he married Emily Barker and began setting down roots in Port Huron. Conger was a busy man between 1854 and 1868, when he was elected to the U.S. House of Representatives. During this period, he practiced law, participated in the organization of the Republican Party and served in the Michigan Senate.

In January 1854, when Stephen A. Douglas proposed the Kansas-Nebraska Act in Congress, abolitionists from the North, who had built themselves up from poverty to a fine station in life, began to feel their freedoms were being encroached on by the slaveholding South. This fired up the movement that had been organizing since the 1820s. The act abolished the Missouri Compromise and instead gave the populace of new states entering the union the choice to be slaveholding or non-slaveholding. It became law on May 30, 1854. Kansas and Nebraska became hotbeds as both pro- and antislavery advocates flooded the territories to sway the vote for or against the issue.

After the Kansas-Nebraska Act was passed, a movement began across the northern states to organize a new national political party. Michigan was one of the first states to organize a convention to address the matter. In June 1854, a conference to oppose the Kansas-Nebraska Act was held at Kalamazoo, Michigan. This organized effort was made up of antislavery Democrats, Free Soilers and Whigs. According to the anonymous author of *Under the Oaks*, the literature drafted at this convention called for an appeal to the people of Michigan and asked them to organize in Jackson, Michigan, on July 6, 1854, to form a new national party called the Republican Party:

> *A great wrong has been perpetrated. The slave power of the Country has triumphed. Liberty is trampled underfoot. The Missouri Compromise, a solemn compact entered into by our Fathers, has been violated and a vast territory, dedicated to freedom, has been opened to slavery.*

This appeal was sent out to members who had attended the conference opposing the Kansas-Nebraska Act in Kalamazoo and to prominent citizens in every county and large town in the state. It was also advertised in all the local Whig and Free Soil newspapers.

THE FIRST REPUBLICAN STATE CONVENTION.

The First Republican State Convention at Jackson, Michigan, 1854, as illustrated in *Zachariah Chandler*, 1880. *Author's Image.*

One of the men who would have received this appeal in the Port Huron area was James W. Sanborn. He was a leading and wealthy lumberman at the time. He was also well connected with other wealthy political men from Detroit, like Zachariah Chandler and Jacob Howard, through his uncle Charles Merrill. We know from the Jackson convention record that Conger attended, James W. Sanborn was appointed to serve as a secretary at the convention, Zachariah Chandler gave an infamous speech there and Jacob Howard was appointed to the committee that drew up a "platform of principles" for the new party.

The convention in Jackson was so large that its activities had to be moved from the convention hall in Jackson to an oak grove on "Morgan's Forty" outside of town. The resolution for the Republican platform created at the convention called the institution of slavery "a moral, social and political evil and a violation of the rights of men" and touched on the repeal of the Missouri Compromise:

> *The recent act of Congress for the creation of the territories Nebraska and Kansas, thus admitting slavery into a region till then sealed against it by*

law, equal in extent to the 13 old states, is an act unprecedented in the history of this country, and one which must engage the earnest and serious attentions of every Northern man.

The platform resolution also called for the repeal of the Fugitive Slave Law of 1850, which required runaway enslaved people who were found in free states to be returned to their enslavers. At the convention, the motto "The North Will Defend You" was adopted by the new Republicans as a show of unity against this law.

After the convention, a committee of delegates was selected, consisting of eighty-eight members who were granted the power to nominate candidates for state office under the new party ticket. James W. Sanborn and Newell Avery were appointed to this committee as representatives from St. Clair County. These members chose the first Republican ticket to run for office in Michigan in the 1855 state elections. Some of the candidates included Kingsley S. Bingham for governor, Jacob Howard for attorney general, Omar Conger for the Michigan Senate and James W. Sanborn for the Michigan House. James's role on the committee of delegates had to play a part in Conger's initial election to office.

Omar Conger was sworn into the Michigan Senate in January 1855. That same year, he also joined the law firm of Edward W. Harris in Port Huron. The firm was known as Harris and Conger. In his recollections of activities in the St. Clair County Circuit Court in 1855, Thomas A.E. Weadock of Bay City remembered Conger as a young attorney at the court, "O.D. Conger was always in attendance upon the courts. He resided in Port Huron and Conger and Mitchell were the two attorneys who tried the most cases in that part of the circuit and they went with the court from one county to the other."

Conger and Sanborn, who were affiliated through personal and business connections, now moved forward as members of the new Republican Party in Michigan. As soon as Conger arrived in Lansing, he introduced the bill to regulate log-running and booming companies. This law was the impetus for *Ames v. The Port Huron Log Driving and Booming Company*, in which Conger provided legal representation for the company, a company James W. Sanborn held an interest in.

THE NATIONAL RISE

Zachariah Chandler, circa 1855–65. *Courtesy of the Library of Congress.*

The first national convention for the Republican Party was held in Pittsburgh on February 22, 1856. A delegation of Michigan men, including Zachariah Chandler and Jacob Howard, attended. Both men were active in the new party, but Chandler was its biggest local advocate, giving speeches across the state of Michigan. On January 10, 1857, Zachariah was voted in by members of the Michigan Legislature as the first Republican from Michigan to take a U.S. Senate seat. His nomination in the Michigan Senate was called on the floor by none other than Omar Conger.

Chandler's victory over Lewis Cass for the U.S. Senate seat was possible through the votes of the members of the new Republican Party in the Michigan Legislature, most notably Thomas W. Ferry, Omar D. Conger and George Jerome. When Chandler went off to Washington, the U.S. House of Representatives was controlled by the Democrats, though ninety-two seats had been won by the new Republican Party. The President was James Buchanan, and the U.S. Supreme Court decision in the Dred Scott case had also just been released. One of the worst decisions in U.S. history, the Dred Scott decision held that enslaved people were not citizens of the United States and thus could expect no protection from the federal government. The decision also stated that Congress had no authority to ban slavery in federal territories. This decision added more fuel to the fire of the antislavery movement. According to the *Detroit Post and Tribune*, Chandler, who was a supporter of John Brown and a critic of the Dred Scott decision, made his opposition known on the Senate floor not long after reaching Washington:

> *What did General Jackson do when the Supreme Court declared the United States Bank constitutional? Did he bow in deference to the opinion of the court? No, he said he would construe the Constitution for himself, that he was sworn to do it. I shall do the same. I have sworn to support the Constitution of the United States, and I have sworn to support it as the fathers made it and not as the Supreme Court have altered it. And I never will swear allegiance to that.*

John Brown and Fellow Raiders Trapped in the Harpers Ferry Amory, 1859. *Courtesy of the Everett Collection/Shutterstock.com.*

At the time Zachariah Chandler was elected to the U.S. Senate, James W. Sanborn and Omar Conger were busy working in the Michigan legislature to address the sales of swamp land. In 1850, Congress had given the governance of swamp lands over to the states. In Michigan, the sales of these lands were issued by the Commissioner of the Land Office. In 1858, James W. Sanborn was elected to this position, an office that wielded great power for a man known in the lumber trade as a land speculator. Sanborn held this position for five years. During his tenure, he was criticized by Democrats for showing favoritism to his nephew, William Sanborn, when he employed him to do work for him in the Michigan Land Office. The criticism was valid. William was in the lumber business and was known to make timberland purchases for his business interests.

HARPERS FERRY

By 1857, John Brown had settled himself in Boston. While there, he began building strong friendships with prominent businessmen from the New England states to raise money to aid an aggressive war taking place in Kansas among pro- and antislavery factions. In 1858, John Brown went to Chatham, Ontario, and drafted a constitution for a slave-free national government. It was in Chatham that Brown began developing an idea to spark a slave revolt in the United States. He believed such a rebellion was the only way to eradicate slavery. While Conger was representing the Port Huron Log Driving and Booming Company in the Michigan Supreme Court, John Brown was getting ready to make his stand and rebel.

On October 16, 1859, under cover of night, Brown and his followers captured Colonel Lewis Washington at his estate west of Harpers Ferry. Washington was a great-grandnephew of George Washington. Brown thought capturing him would grab people's attention. That same evening, Brown and his men also managed to cut the telegraph wire to the city and seize a train that was passing through town. They all spent the night at the armory. They were discovered the next morning by army workers. A company of local militia surrounded the armory, and a gun assault followed, killing four residents. John Brown and his party were confined to the armory as more militia poured into the city. By late afternoon, President James Buchanan had ordered the U.S. Marines to get involved under the command of Colonel Robert E. Lee. The marines arrived on October 18. Brown's company was issued a warning to surrender. They chose to fight. The result was a forced assault that lasted three minutes and caused the deaths of many of Brown's men. Those who were not killed in the skirmish were captured, including Brown. John Brown was tried in Charles Town, found guilty of treason and hanged on December 2. This rebellion caused a great stir among the American people and was said to be the prelude to the Civil War.

In April 1860, a young man, Franklin Benjamin Sanborn, a distant cousin of James, Cummings, John P. and William Sanborn, was approached by Federal Marshals at his home in Concord, Massachusetts. They wanted to take him to Washington to testify before the U.S. Senate regarding his involvement with John Brown. The federal government believed him to be one of the Secret Six, who were said to have funded John Brown's abolitionist escapades in Kansas and Harpers Ferry. Franklin had become acquainted with John Brown in his youth and was devoted to the freedom of those enslaved in the South and the emancipation of the North. He became active in the defense of Kansas in 1855. Franklin never did face the U.S. Senate. On the day the marshals came for him, members of his local community drew up a writ of habeas corpus in his name. The matter was heard by Chief Justice Shaw. The federal marshal's attempt to take Franklin was declared unlawful, and he was released. After that, the federal government left Franklin alone.

Franklin became a well-known scholar, author and journalist in his time. He wrote biographies about many of his famous friends, including Henry David Thoreau and Ralph Waldo Emerson. In 1885, he also penned *Life and Letters of John Brown*. According to V.C. Sanborn, Franklin's manuscript journal, the *Star of Social Reform*, also makes mentions of John Brown: "I was also making my first experiments in love, without forming any serious connection, until, in my nineteenth year, it was my good fortune to meet the person who had the most inspiring influence on that portion of my life which preceded my acquaintance with Emerson and John Brown. This was Miss Ariana Smith Walker, a grandniece of Webster's witty friend, Judge Smith of Exeter."

THE FIRST REPUBLICAN IN THE WHITE HOUSE

The Kansas-Nebraska Act, the Dred Scott decision and the hanging of John Brown were events that unsettled American citizens and fueled negative discourse between the North and South. By the time Abraham Lincoln won the presidential election in 1860, talk of secession had reached a boiling point. By December, South Carolina had seceded from the Union. By January 1861, six other slaveholding states seceded: Mississippi, Florida, Alabama, Georgia, Louisiana and Texas. A month after Lincoln took office, in April 1861, the Civil War began.

When Lincoln took office, Senate Republicans reorganized the Committee of Commerce, and Zachariah Chandler served as its chairman in Washington. Chandler's status on this committee was instrumental in funding the ship canal project in the St. Clair Flats. In Michigan, Omar Conger was appointed to the State Military Board, which was involved in the oversight of sending men and supplies to aid the war effort. While Conger worked to supply men for the war, Chandler spent his time meeting the Michigan troops as they arrived in Washington. He personally met the first regiment of Michigan volunteers at the train station and purchased supplies for them out of his own funds to ensure they were well cared for.

THE ASSASSINATION OF LINCOLN
AND EVERTON J. CONGER

Omar Conger's brother Everton served and fought in the Civil War. After he was injured twice in battle while serving in the Eighth Ohio Infantry, he was given a commission to serve in the First District of Columbia Cavalry in 1863. The First District of Columbia Cavalry was a mounted force used by Lafayette Charles Baker's new secret service group created under the Lincoln administration. This force was also called Baker's Mounted Rangers and was commanded by Lafayette's cousin Luther B. Baker. According to Rob Wick, on Everton's arrival to his new post, Luther B. Baker commented, "Lt. Col. Everton J. Conger came into the regiment at about that time to take charge while Col. L.C. Baker continued on detached service with the Detective Bureau of Washington. Conger already had a significant army record. I believe it was by political influence that he obtained his appointment in our regiment." While it was suggested this appointment was influenced by Omar Conger, no records exist to support this claim.

Both brothers proved to be champions of the antislavery cause: Omar through speech and Everton through action. While Everton was serving in his new unit, he was sent to retrieve a Union soldier who was being held in a Maryland prison. When he arrived at the prison, he found formerly enslaved people being held in jail with the servicemen. He asked the men why they were being held. The men responded they were being held to be kept from leaving. Everton demanded the formerly enslaved men be freed along with the soldier and stated: "You are all free and may go when and where you want to." When Everton made ready to leave the town, he encountered the formerly enslaved being held by a group of men on the outskirts of town. He ordered the men to let them pass. They did not comply with his request. Everton threatened the men that he would take them by force to Washington if they did not step aside. He said: "God only knows when you will get back. You know, or ought to know, that the Emancipation Proclamation has been issued and you have no more right to hold these people than you have to hold me." The men were released and allowed to leave the town.

In 1865, after Lincoln's assassination, Everton was one of the men deployed to capture John Wilkes Booth. He is said to have set fire to the barn in Virginia where Booth was hiding and was present when Booth was captured and killed. It is ironic that almost six years after John Brown was

Planning the Capture of Booth, 1865. *From left to right*: Lieutenant L.B. Baker, Colonel L.C. Baker, E.J. Conger. *Courtesy of the Metropolitan Museum of Art.*

hanged, Booth, who was present at his hanging, would find himself on the run for the assassination of Lincoln and later captured and killed in the presence of Omar Conger's brother. The world can be small sometimes.

RADICAL APPOINTMENT

After the war, James W. Sanborn and other influential Republicans in Port Huron approached Chandler to urge him to use his influence in Washington to create and establish a new customs district in Port Huron. Prior to the war, the customs office fell under the jurisdiction of Detroit. James W. Sanborn's nephew, William Sanborn, served as the deputy collector for Port Huron until 1862, when he entered the army to fight for the Union cause. His brother John P. Sanborn took over and held the deputy collector position for the next four years. At the time the idea for a new customs district was conceived, John P. Sanborn was hopeful he would be appointed the new Collector of Customs.

Chandler was successful in helping his fellow Republicans in Port Huron with their request. On March 20, 1866, a bill was introduced on the Senate floor as Bill S. 199 to create a customs office in Port Huron to be known as the District of Huron. On April 12, 1866, Chandler, as a member of the Commerce Committee, brought the amendments from the House on the bill to the Senate floor. The bill passed, and it was signed by President Andrew Johnson on April 13. The new law was recorded on the floor of the Senate on April 16. However, getting John P. Sanborn appointed was not as easy as passing the bill. President Johnson refused to appoint John P. Sanborn to the position because he was a Radical Republican. Instead, he nominated John Atkinson. John went to work immediately displacing J.P. Sanborn, but Congress would not approve John's appointment. Instead, Chandler fought tirelessly for John P. Sanborn to be appointed and advised his colleagues to reject President Johnson's nomination.

Knowing he would never be appointed as the Collector of Customs, on February 9, 1867, Atkinson wrote to President Johnson to secure the nomination of Edgar G. Spaulding, a fellow customs agent working in the office. Edgar was the nephew of Charlotte Fish Sanborn, the widow of Cummings Sanborn and second wife to James W. Sanborn. Regarding Edgar's nomination, Atkinson stated:

> *I have the honor to enclose the application of Edgar G. Spaulding asking to be appointed Collector of Customs at Port Huron to fill a vacancy occasioned by my rejection. Mr. Spaulding is a young man of ability and integrity. He was a gallant soldier and is thoroughly acquainted with his duties as a Revenue Officer. He will be confirmed by the senate if nominated. Of this there is no room for doubt. He has never been active*

as a politician but has authorized me to speak for him in saying that he will give your policy an honest support. The Congressional delegation will present John P. Sanborn, William Sanborn, or John W. Thompson. They are all bitter political enemies of yourself and the two Sanborns have been bitter personal assailants. Those who have yielded your policy an honest and hearty support Democrats and Republicans alike ask as a special favor to them that neither John P. Sanborn nor William Sanborn be appointed.

President Johnson nominated Spaulding, but the Senate rejected him on February 25. Two days later, President Johnson caved and nominated John P. Sanborn, whom the U.S. Senate confirmed on March 2, 1867. As J.P. Sanborn and Chandler battled for the customs appointment, Conger's star began to shine politically. His appointment as a member of the committee to revise the state constitution in 1867 allowed him the opportunity to express his views on voting rights for African Americans. Conger, a known advocate for human rights for all people, remarked, "The negro is just as much a citizen of the United States today, by the supreme law of the land, as is the gentleman himself; he is just as much a citizen of the United States as I am or as any member of this Convention is." In discussions about adding language to differentiate between the races of people and voting privileges, Conger stated:

Why throw upon a class of citizens, whom he claims to desire to see voters in this State, that old long dishonored brand and stigma of disgrace, by calling them "black," or speaking of the others as "white?" Why make any distinction of races, if the gentleman is in favor of all legal citizens of the United States, of proper age and sex, voting in this State? I tell you there can be no mistake in regard to the object of this proposition. There are those of us who desire that our new Constitution shall extend the right of suffrage to all legal citizens entitled to it, without distinction of race. Why should we make that distinction at all between men entitled to vote, except for the absurd and unfounded prejudice which has rankled in the hearts of men from generation to generation until now, and which even the power of Almighty God it seems cannot drive from the hearts of men, although they will admit these men to be citizens?

Since Conger was a founding member of the Republican Party in Michigan and a friend of James W. Sanborn, it is no surprise that in July 1868, he was nominated to run for a seat in the U.S. House of Representatives by the fellow party members of his district. At the time, the Fifth District was represented by delegates from St. Clair, Macomb, Livingston, Lapeer, Sanilac and Oakland Counties. At the convention, James W. Sanborn presided over the meeting as president, and it was Major Nathan S. Boynton who nominated Omar Conger. The delegate for Oakland County nominated the incumbent, R.E. Trowbridge. Conger won the day with fourteen votes, and in the fall of 1868, he won the district seat in the U.S. House of Representatives.

SERVICE AND MEMORY

Omar Conger would go on to represent Michigan in the U.S. House until 1881, when he was elected for one term to the U.S. Senate. During his time in Congress, he served on the Committee on Expenditures in the Department of State, the Committee on Patents, the Committee on the Revision of the Laws, the Committee on Post Office and Post Roads and as Chairman on the Committee on Manufactures.

Conger's terms in federal office greatly benefited the Port Huron area. While in office, Conger is credited with the building of the U.S. Customs House, which still stands proudly on Water Street, and with effectuating and negotiating for the sale of the military reservation property and for the creation of Pine Grove Park. After Conger lost his seat in the U.S. Senate, he lived out his remaining years in Washington. After his death in 1898, Conger finally returned home to Port Huron to be buried in Lakeside Cemetery.

All politicians rise and fall, but very few remain celebrated historically. Omar Conger is one of the exceptions. According to the *Yale Expositor*, James G. Blaine, one of Conger's Washington friends and former Speaker of the House, paid the following tribute to Conger in his book *Twenty Years in Congress*:

> *Omar D. Conger of Michigan was a well trained debater before he entered the house, and at once took a prominent part in its deliberations. He illustrated the virtue of persistence in its highest decree and had the art of annoying an opponent to the point of torture. I remember well in after years when I became Journal Clerk of the house, how he stood like the rock of Chickamauga against the Democratic hosts. Particularly well do I remember how he met and unhorsed Sam Cox, how he bowled down Sam Randall, Beck, Proctor, Knott, Joe Blackburn, Randolph Tucker, General*

Omar Dwight Conger, circa 1860–75. *Courtesy of the Library of Congress.*

Hutton and other Democratic leaders and how his leadership was almost invariably followed by the rank and file of the Republican Party. He was a stalwart of stalwarts. But he especially excelled in his knowledge of the rules and of pending legislation. I say with thorough knowledge of the subject during all of his congressional and senatorial career that no member from Michigan ever equaled his work or record.

KING JOHN

One of the most provocative pioneers of St. Clair County was John Pitts (J.P.) Sanborn. He was known for being dominant in local and state Republican political circles, where he was often referred to as "King John." He was a risk-taker drawn to capitalist ventures and a man of strong will who often found himself embroiled in controversial situations. He was the oldest son of Dr. Benjamin Sanborn and Emeline Pitts of Falmouth, Maine, and was born in 1833. His father and James W. Sanborn were brothers, both born to Dr. William Sanborn and Nancy Merrill.

Before J.P. stepped foot into Michigan, he was well connected through family in the Detroit and Port Huron areas. His uncles were James W. Sanborn and Charles Merrill. J.P. was related to Merrill through his grandmother Nancy Merrill. Charles and his grandmother were siblings. J.P. was also related to Merrill through his aunt and Charles's wife, Frances Pitts. Frances Pitts was his mother's sister. This relationship made Charles and Frances Pitts Merrill's daughter, Lizzie Pitts Merrill, J.P.'s cousin. Lizzie eventually married Thomas W. Palmer of Detroit, who was Charles Merrill's business partner. These family relationships gave J.P. a prosperous start in Michigan. He came to Michigan in 1847, after his father died to work in the mercantile and lumber industries under his uncles, James W. Sanborn and Charles Merrill. He eventually settled in Port Huron and married Mary A. Wastell in 1855. During the Civil War, he was unable to serve as a soldier. When his brother, William Sanborn, went off to serve in the war, J.P. took over his position as deputy collector of the customs office.

THE POWER OF APPOINTMENT

After the war, James W. Sanborn's political ties and friendship with Zachariah Chandler assisted in the creation of a new customs post at Port Huron, and J.P. was appointed the first collector in 1867. Civil appointments were pretty much controlled by the U.S. Senators in those days, even though the power of appointment belonged to the President of the United States. It was common practice and custom for the President to bend the knee and allow Senators to dictate his appointments. The Senators used their appointment-making to gain and keep power within their local and state congressional districts. Zachariah Chandler was a major Republican powerhouse in Michigan and Washington. J.P. Sanborn served as the Collector of Customs for the Port Huron District from 1867 until March 1883.

A sketch portrait of John P. Sanborn, as illustrated in *Genealogy of the Family of Samborne or Sanborn in England and America 1194–1898. Courtesy of Family Search.*

While the political connections J.P. garnered through James W. Sanborn jump-started his political power locally when he was granted the customs position initially, it was the continuous collectorship appointment to the position that followed that gave J.P. power over local members of the Republican Party after the death of his uncle, James W. Sanborn. The only federal appointments at the time in St. Clair County were the Collector and the Postmaster positions. Out of the two, the collectorship was more financially and politically lucrative. Back when J.P. served in the position, the United States government did not have an income tax system. It used tariffs, such as import fees, to fund the government. The income J.P. earned was tied to the amount of money the customhouse brought in. Port Huron was a busy shipping port back in those days. Serving in the position, J.P. Sanborn became quite wealthy. In addition to his income from the customhouse, J.P. also earned income from two wealthy estates acting as the trustee for the James W. Sanborn and Mary Sweetser's estates after 1870.

PRELUDE TO THE COLLECTORSHIP CONTROVERSY

The only drawback of the collectorship position was its dependency on senatorial appointment. Luckily, Chandler, who gave J.P. his original appointment as a favor to his uncle, continued to subsequently reappoint him. Senator Chandler was always agreeable to sign a recommendation to the President for J.P. Sanborn. The two men shared a warm friendship until Chandler's death in 1879. After Chandler's death, J.P. needed to find a new senatorial relationship to keep his appointment. Was Omar Conger that man? It is well recorded in Port Huron history that John P. Sanborn was the man who took Omar Conger from the U.S. House to the U.S. Senate and then out of politics altogether after serving only one term in the U.S. Senate. There may be some truth to these statements, but is it the whole story?

By 1879, the Republican Party was experiencing political difficulties. Cronyism, or the spoils system, was common practice. Various factions developed in response, causing friction within the party. Those who supported cronyism were called Stalwarts. Senators Roscoe Conkling of New York and Chandler of Detroit were known Stalwarts. Those who wanted to create a new merit-based system for civil appointments were called Half-Breeds. Senator James G. Blaine of Maine was a known Half-Breed. Given Conger's relationship with Blaine, it is probable Conger subscribed to some of the Half-Breeds' beliefs, although he has never been historically identified with either faction.

These two factions caused much infighting within the party. The party, which had dominated for seventeen years, became vulnerable, as Democrats started to regained strength across the country. The 1876 Presidential Election of Republican Rutherford B. Hayes was almost lost. The gold standard and tariffs on imports were issues that politically divided the country. The Republicans' power and control of the country were in jeopardy, and it was well known among the rank-and-file members of the party that the 1880 election would be a close one.

As the party began losing its footing, Chandler passed away. J.P., William Hartsuff, Fred Wells and Henry Howard attended his funeral in Detroit. Chandler's vacancy in the U.S. Senate called for the Michigan Governor to appoint someone to fill his seat until the next election. Henry B. Baldwin was appointed. As the 1880 elections approached, local men began to talk about Conger's U.S. House seat and nominating someone new from the district to run instead of Conger. Conger had retained the seat since 1869. There was also talk of Conger being nominated to Chandler's seat in the U.S. Senate, which Conger openly opposed because he did not want to cause discord among his fellow party members. But as the 1880 Republican National Convention approached, this talk continued. Conger was chosen by the members of his local party district as a delegate to the convention. On May 8, 1880, the *Port Huron Daily Times* praised Conger's selection as a delegate: "Who can represent the Republicans of Michigan better than Mr. Conger? Untrammeled by the claims of factions, unbounded by personal pledges, an ardent admirer of Michigan's preference why not select Mr. Conger? With Omar D. Conger as chairman of the Michigan delegation it at once takes a responsible and honorable position in the national convention."

THE 1880 REPUBLICAN NATIONAL CONVENTION

All the members of the Republican Party were aware going into the 1880 Republican National Convention that trouble was brewing between competing factions and that nominations might prove difficult. The favored candidates were former President Grant, Senator James G. Blaine, Treasury Secretary John Sherman and Senator George F. Edmunds. While Grant did not actively promote his candidacy, his entry in the race energized the Stalwart faction of the party. The delegates at the convention were immediately polarized into two camps and were labeled either Grant delegates or anti-Grant delegates. The Michigan delegates entered the convention as known Blaine supporters or anti-Grant delegates. Michigan's James Frederick Joy nominated Blaine and gave a speech on his behalf at the convention. The arrival of Michigan's delegates in Chicago was noted by the *Port Huron Daily News* under the headline "Michigan News" on June 2, 1880:

> There was a great influx of Michigan people this morning and there are probably more visitors on the ground from Michigan than any state except Illinois. The rooms are handsomely decorated with flags, portraits of Blaine, etc., and have been more crowded all day than those of any other state. The delegation has been active and earnest. Mr. Joy and Mr. Conger have both exerted a large influence and have been summoned to frequent consultations.

Special homage was paid to the late Michigan U.S. Senator Zachariah Chandler via the décor at the convention. The hall featured a large oil

A photograph of James G. Blaine, 1870s. *Courtesy of the Everett Collection/ Shutterstock.com.*

painting and a life-size plastered bust of him. The painting was prominently placed over the convention chairman's desk and invoked the memory of Chandler's dedicated service to the party. Reporting on the arrangement of the hall, the *Port Huron Daily Times* wrote, "Everywhere Mr. Chandler is spoken of with respect and expressions of regret are heard on every hand. In the headquarters of a dozen states I have heard the remark made 'If Chandler had lived, he would have been the nominee of the convention for he was the stalwart of stalwarts upon whom we could have united the party most easily.'"

During the convention, very little business was conducted during the first few days, as excitement and rumors spread among the factions of the party. Senator Conkling from New York and Senator Logan from Illinois, both Grant supporters and Stalwart members, tried to exert their influence and spoke confidently on his nomination. The issue of delegate representation at the convention and how they were chosen was discussed. Some of the local congressional districts' delegation appointments for the states of Alabama, Illinois, Kansas, Utah and Louisiana had been overturned by their state conventions. New pro-Grant delegates were chosen to replace the local delegates so that these five states would only send pro-Grant supporters to the National Convention. The unit rule in the party dictated local district delegate selection practice. A reporter from the *Chicago Tribune* asked Conger about his thoughts on the rule. Conger responded:

> *My belief is that there should be no effort made to prevent direct representation from the people and the only way to subserve this end is to permit the district delegates to obey the wishes of their constituents. There should be no attempt to defeat the will of the people and I believe that anything that tends in that direction will be defeated. Let the state conventions elect the delegates at large and the districts the district delegations and we shall surely have full and free expression of the wishes of the people.*

Omar Conger was selected to serve on the Committee on Credentials at the National Convention and was chosen its chairman. This committee was assigned to investigate the unit rule controversy and issue its findings on the matter. Comments and speculations circulating on the issue were reported by the *Port Huron Daily Times*:

> *As it is well understood that one of the hardest fights in the convention will be over the seats more especially concerning the Illinois contest upon the settlement of which will depend the question of district representation not only for this but future conventions. As well, the Michigan delegation selected Judge Conger to represent them where his extended knowledge of precedents and fighting qualities will make him very useful. Mr. Conger was made chairman of the committee on credentials as it was expected he would be in view of his ability and prominence.*

On June 4, 1880, the committee met and issued a report of its decision on the unit rule controversy. Its decision was to allow the delegate seats originally chosen by their districts to stand and participate in the National Convention. The delegates chosen to replace them by state conventions were overturned and dismissed. The rationale for the committee's decision was simple. Since the organization of the party in 1856, delegates for the National Convention had always been chosen by the local districts. The committee saw no reason to change that practice or amend it. Senator Logan from Illinois objected to the report. According to the *Port Huron Daily Times*'s coverage on the report of the committee dated on June 5, Conger took the floor to defend the actions of the committee in response to Logan's objection:

> *Sir, I make no apology to the grand state of Illinois for having reported that their chosen citizens had a right to be here. No, sir and I make no apology to this grand convention and this vast concourse of citizens of the United States that I preside over a committee that had the moral courage to say to the world and sir not only do I take the responsibility, but it is delightful to me to point this convention to the time honored usage of that party which believes in the absolute equality of citizenship and the absolute equality of all members of a National Republican convention.*

The committee report was adopted, and the matter was closed. Conger's handling of the issue was hailed with praise June 7, 1880, in the *Port Huron Daily Times*:

> *During the long day and stormy night no man in the convention appeared to better advantage than the Hon. Omar D. Conger. His report is agreed on all hands, even by those who disagree with his conclusion to be a clear forcible and logical document. Standing on the front of the platform with the vast audience before him, his tones penetrated the remotest recesses of the great building and it was evident as he went on that he was carrying the crowd with him. In the parliamentary struggle that followed he was always strong stating his points clearly and ending every time with the best end of the string. Michiganders were charmed. He won laurels for himself and his state. His name today is on every tongue and all agree that he was the best loaded and did the surest shooting of any of the big guns in the fight.*

Over the course of the next few days, balloting commenced without producing a nominee. Grant was backed by the Stalwarts, Blaine by the Half-Breeds and Sherman by those who were not of either faction. At one point in the balloting, James Garfield was given a few votes. Blaine and Sherman knew they could not win, so they decided to begin negotiating with the anti-Grant voters to switch their votes to Garfield. Conger went to Garfield's room at 2:39 a.m. and told him he thought he just might be voted in for the presidential nomination. Garfield responded that he was loyal to Sherman and felt that his friends were doing him an injustice by trying to negotiate votes for him. By the thirty-fifth ballot, the Blaine and Sherman votes had switched over to Garfield, and on the thirty-sixth ballot, Garfield won the nomination with 399 votes. The delegates gathered around Garfield as the dark horse winner. A band began playing, and everyone started singing "The Battle Cry of Freedom."

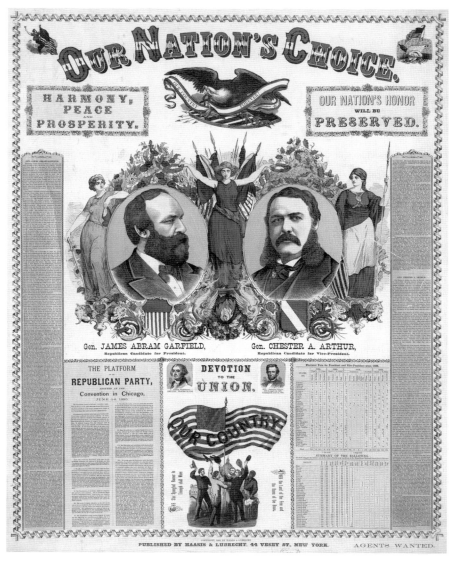

Our Nation's Choice: a campaign poster for Garfield and Arthur, circa 1880. *Courtesy of the Library of Congress.*

Conger was one of the men who accompanied Garfield on his victory ride home from the convention, traveling as far as Alliance, Ohio, with him. On the journey, it was reported that Conger conversed with Blaine about his loss, and Blaine was more than agreeable about Garfield's nomination.

Senator Cameron from Pennsylvania also traveled with the group and expressed his confidence in Garfield's victory in November. Garfield was met by enthusiastic crowds as he made his way back home to northern Ohio.

A Victory for Garfield and Conger

The 1880 Presidential Election that November was a close one. Garfield ran against two opponents: General Winfield Scott Hancock of the Democratic Party and James B. Weaver, a congressman from Iowa. Weaver was the candidate for the newly formed Greenbacks Party, a left-wing upstart. To solidify his victory, Garfield had to negotiate with the Stalwart leader of New York, Senator Roscoe Conkling. He was to meet Conkling at the Fifth Avenue Hotel in New York that August. However, Conkling stood him up and sent Chester Arthur to meet with him instead. In exchange for the New York vote, Arthur informed Garfield that Conkling demanded he be allowed to retain his senatorial power of appointment. He especially wanted to keep the appointment for the Collector of the Customs House position. At the time, New York's customhouse brought in about 70 to 80 percent of all U.S. imports and accounted for about one-third of the country's revenue. There is no written account of the meeting. But in later conversations, Conkling told others that Garfield agreed in that meeting with Arthur to give him complete control over the New York's customhouse appointment. After Garfield's compromise with Conklin, he won the presidency by a slim margin. His victory was ensured by a mere 1,898 votes over Hancock.

Also, that November, Conger's name was put forth by the local members of the Port Huron Republican Party as a candidate to fill Chandler's Michigan U.S. Senate seat. The members who campaigned for his nomination in the Michigan Legislature were General William Hartsuff, Fred L. Wells, C.F. Harrington, J.P. Sanborn and Judge C.R. Brown. At the Michigan Legislative Caucus, held on January 6, 1881, Conger was nominated to the seat along with John J. Bagley and Henry P. Baldwin. On the first ballot, Conger had thirty-two votes, with Bagley leading with forty-three and Baldwin trailing with forty. On the sixth ballot, Baldwin's name was withdrawn. The seventh ballot thus determined the win, with the final tally being Conger, fifty-nine; Bagley, fifty-seven; and J.J. Woodman, one. Conger won the seat to the U.S. Senate by a mere two votes.

Honorable senator Omar Dwight Conger of Michigan, circa 1865–80. *Courtesy of the Library of Congress.*

The *Port Huron Times* celebrated his nomination and victory on June 6, 1881:

> *We believe the Republicans of the state may well congratulate themselves on Mr. Conger's nomination. Without detracting at all from the merits of rival aspirants for the position, we may fairly claim now, as we have heretofore that Mr. Conger's long service in the House, as well as state legislative bodies, and his clearly proved natural ability as a legislator, place him above all others in point of merit; and we have no doubt that in his senatorial career he will reflect honor upon himself, and upon the great state he will represent. We have won the victory. We have won it honorably and fairly and although the unsuccessful candidates and their friends will doubtless feel keen disappointment, no ill feeling will remain, and all will acquiesce cheerfully in the result.*

Without a doubt, Conger's rise to notoriety at the 1880 Republican National Convention and his friendship with the newly elected President Garfield placed him as the frontrunner for the seat. With other locals calling for his House seat, Conger's move to the Senate came at the right time for him politically. It is possible the Port Huron membership's canvassing efforts on Conger's behalf helped him, but contrary to past reporting, it was not the sole reason for his ascendancy to the U.S. Senate. Regardless, with Conger's old ties to J.P.'s uncle James W. Sanborn, Conger's senatorial appointment must have given J.P. confidence Conger would allow him to keep the customhouse appointment. What J.P. could not have anticipated were the events that followed Conger's appointment and Garfield's win and how those events would impact the Republican Party.

Time for a Change

President Garfield was not a member of either faction in the Republican Party, but he agreed with the Half-Breeds that civil service reform in Washington was needed. He felt appointments should be based on merit and skill sets, not friendships. However, when he took office, he immediately bent the knee to Senator Conkling and put through some of the appointments he demanded. But by May 1881, Garfield had grown tired of Conkling's demands. He decided he would not be dictated to any longer. When it came time to choose the appointment for the Collector of the New York Customs House, Garfield did not nominate Conkling's man. Instead, he chose his own nominee, William H. Robertson. He defended his nomination by asserting his executive right to appointment. Thus, a battle between presidential preference and senatorial courtesy began on Capitol Hill.

In reaction to Garfield's appointment, Conkling asked for a Senatorial Caucus to meet and discuss the matter with the President. Members of the party agreed to form the caucus. They spoke to Garfield on Conkling's behalf for over two hours. Garfield was asked to withdraw Robertson, and the members reminded him of the practice of senatorial courtesy in making appointments. Garfield refused, stating that he wanted to keep harmony within the party but that he would not be threatened. After the caucus, President Garfield told his closest confidants that any senator who stood in the way of the appointment would be barred from his office for the remainder of his term. Despite the President's threat, Conkling was confident Robertson would not be confirmed. He kept pressure on his friends in Congress. Conkling's defiance was criticized by a friend of President Garfield in the press on May 7:

For many years Mr. Conkling has made open war on every Republican in and out of his state who would not bend the knee at his imperious will; and although President Garfield signalized his entry into office by appointing one of Conkling's intimate friends to a position in his cabinet, and by numerous appointments of Conkling's followers to important offices in the state of New York nothing would satisfy the New York Senator but the complete surrender to him of the patronage of New York and complete ignoring of the large Republican element in the state that is hostile to him. This the President could not do without turning his back on the men whose action rendered his own nomination and election possible and without a complete surrender of the Presidential prerogative of appointment.

To prove he meant business, Garfield pressed Conkling further. He withdrew some of the prior nominations for the southern and eastern districts of New York. This infuriated Conkling. He retaliated by asking his colleagues to withhold the votes on confirming all appointments before Congress. His party members complied. A few days later, another caucus was put together to discuss the issue. Conkling did not attend. The members discussed the nomination and confirmation issue. To circumvent the Robertson nomination, it was suggested Congress only confirm existing vacancies. They found this solution unworkable, as it would leave too many vacancies open in the Federal Government and no work would get done. Some members of the caucus felt that Garfield's actions were infringing on senatorial business.

Roscoe Conkling, a U.S. senator from New York. *Courtesy of Morphart Creation/ Shutterstock.com.*

Other members admitted they were being pressured by New York Stalwarts to dispose of Mr. Robertson. Several of Conkling's friends had come to Washington to urge him to let the nomination be reported without recommendation to appease the President and keep the peace in the party. Rumors began so spread that Conkling said the President had deceived him with the Robertson appointment. Conkling denied the accusations. Members in the caucus decided it would be wise to approach President Garfield to make sure he understood these were merely rumors and assure him that Conkling was not threatening or attempting to defame him. They thought that if Garfield was made to understand this, he might be willing to compromise.

After much debate, the caucus determined that Robertson's appointment would be confirmed. It was agreed Conger would report the nomination without any recommendation, and the nomination would be held until Conkling could make a speech citing his rationale for opposing the confirmation. After the Conkling speech, a vote would be held. Conkling responded angrily by insinuating the caucus had been held behind his back, and he declared it an attempt to defeat him by indirect methods. He threatened that Robertson's confirmation would defeat the Republican Party in New York. Later that day, Conkling and fellow New York Senator Platt resigned from the Senate. The resignation letter delivered to members of the Senate by Vice President Chester Arthur on May 17 read, "Sir, will you please announce to the senate that my resignation as a senator of the United States from the state of New York has been forwarded to the governor of the state?"

This news created intense excitement throughout Washington. Crowds collected on the streets, and gossip was rampant. It was implied Conkling was confident he would be reappointed by the New York Legislature, despite his resignation. The President did not react with surprise. He indicated that he was prepared for the news, and he felt Conkling was in a weak position he could not meet. He said that instead of accepting his defeat, he resigned. Garfield stood behind his nomination. General Grant wrote to the President on Conkling's behalf and shared his willingness to stand behind him. Others questioned whether the resignations were valid. In the end, Conkling and Platt were not reappointed, and Robertson was confirmed. This affair ended Conkling's Stalwart reign of power in the Senate. He never regained his political career or his power.

SHOTS IN THE TRAIN DEPOT

To the victor go the spoils. However, for President Garfield, this was not the case. Not long after the Conkling dispute, Garfield was shot in the Baltimore and Potomac Railroad Station in Washington. On July 2, 1881, he was in the station with James G. Blaine and his two sons. They were leaving the city for their summer vacation. Lincoln's son, Robert Todd Lincoln, who was serving as Garfield's Secretary of War, was waiting at the station to see him off. In those days, Presidents did not travel with security. As Garfield entered the station, he was shot by Charles J. Guiteau. A policeman on the scene

The scene of the assassination of President James A. Garfield, 1881. *Courtesy of the Everett Collection/Shutterstock.com.*

captured Guiteau. When asked why he shot the President, Guiteau stated that he was a Stalwart and wanted Chester Arthur to be President.

President Garfield was shot twice. He lingered in sickness for the next few months, suffering from infections caused by his wounds. He died on September 19, 1881. Vice President Chester Arthur was sworn in as President of the United States on September 22, 1881. Later, it was proved Guiteau believed a speech he had written on behalf of Garfield was responsible for Garfield's narrow victory over Scott in the presidential election. Because of this, he convinced himself Garfield owed him a position in his administration. On more than one occasion, he had approached Garfield, Blaine and other members of the President's Cabinet to make his claim. Eventually, he was banned from the White House. This banning prompted Guiteau to shoot the President. Guiteau was put on trial and executed by hanging on June 30, 1882.

A few months after the President's passing, the members of the Senate passed a resolution to create a committee to consider how to remember and honor their deceased president. This committee, comprised of eight senators, selected Omar Conger to serve alongside one of Garfield's closest friends, John Sherman to decide how best to honor and pay tribute to President Garfield's service.

CIVIL SERVICE REFORM:
THE FERRY/COLLECTORSHIP CONTROVERSIES

Because of the circumstances surrounding Garfield's death, the push for civil service reform gained momentum. Initially, the concept of reform had been introduced under the Haynes administration in 1880 by Ohio Senator George H. Pendleton. The bill he proposed created a merit-based system that would require candidates to submit to an examination to replace party cronyism. Pendleton's bill did not pass in 1880. But by late 1881, public outcry over Garfield's death led to the creation of the National Civil Service Reform League, and a major campaign for reform was instituted by members of the general public. This league publicly argued the old spoils system was a contributing factor in Garfield's death. This prompted President Arthur to call for reform in his first congressional address, and Democrats running for office in the 1882 elections campaigned on civil service reform. The party gained seats in the election, and for the first time in a long time, the Democrats held a majority in the House of Representatives. Their loss of House seats prompted more Republicans to take up the civil service cause. In the fall of 1882, Pendleton reintroduced a civil service reform bill in Congress.

Conger gave a big speech on the Senate floor regarding the Pendleton Bill on December 21, 1882, as reported by the *Port Huron Daily Times* on December 28, 1882:

> *We have been here day after day for a week past the time of the senate consumed in long rambling discussions about the civil service of the country and the passage of a civil service bill. Sir, the people of this country if they read the record, will see it bristling with speeches from gentlemen on the other side of the house, professing great love for civil service reform, an anxiety unconcealed, an earnestness unpressed, to have some measure passed which shall redeem the civil service of the country from its imperfections and its faults. I am in favor of some bill of this kind for years [sic]. I have noted to appropriate money and give the President money with which he could institute his commission and make his inquiries and carry-on civil service reform in the country. It is no new zeal, no new interest, that I feel in the subject. What the particular measure shall be I do not know. In fact, any measure that looks to the desirable end I am willing to join with the senator from Ohio in pressing forward; and I come to his help the more readily and the more earnestly because I sympathize with him, standing alone in the camp of the enemy and holding up a flag around which none of his fellow's rally.*

On December 28, 1882, the Pendleton Bill was passed by an emphatic vote. Conger was a "yea." As civil service reform was given lip service and support from an ideological standpoint by both political parties across the country, two controversies were brewing simultaneously in Michigan. They started in the late fall of 1882 and heated up after the New Year in 1883. These two controversies overlapped and tested whether members of the Michigan Republican Party were ready to adapt to the changes of civil service reform they so readily aspired to verbally support and give up the cronyism in their ranks. In both instances, the party failed. The party did vote in two new candidates to evidence its support of reform. But behind closed doors, what it did was merely exchange one power for another, proving old habits die hard. The outcome of both events was the downfall of Senator Conger and the cause of the loss of his seat in Congress in 1887. The two events became known as the Ferry and Custom House Controversies. J.P. Sanborn and his friends in the local district, while not solely responsible for Conger's demise, would prove to be willing participants in the scheme.

While Congress was debating the Pendleton Bill in late 1882, members of the Michigan Republican delegation were considering the reelection of Michigan U.S. Senator Ferry on a state level, and J.P. Sanborn's collectorship was getting ready to expire on a local level. Considering civil service reform and Sanborn's long-standing appointment as Collector of the Custom House for the Port Huron District, Conger found himself in a precarious position. He was faced with choosing between his Republican political interests in Washington, where he was displaying his support for reform, and his interests in Port Huron politics, where he kept Sanborn happy with a reappointment. The timing could not have been worse for him. William Hartsuff, the current Postmaster in Port Huron, wanted the collectorship, so he set out to use Conger's vulnerable position and Senator Ferry's reelection to his advantage.

The beginning of the contest between Hartsuff and Sanborn was first reported in the *Port Huron Daily Times* on November 24, 1882, just weeks after Senator Ferry campaigned in Port Huron to generate Republican votes in the 1882 midterm election: "William Hartsuff has received the endorsement of Senators Conger and Ferry for appointment as collector of customs at this port and it is expected that the congressional delegation will also sign his recommendation to the President. The appointment is to be made on the expiration of Mr. Sanborn's term, next February or March."

In a week, the contest was in full swing locally. On December 2, 1882, the *Port Huron Daily Times* reported:

The contest for the collectorship of this port seems to be gathering strength from day to day and is extending throughout the district. In this city, a remonstrance against the appointment of Gen. Hartsuff has been circulated and also a petition for the reappointment of Mr. Sanborn, but how extensively they have been signed we are not informed. In other parts of the district representatives of both parties have been at work and we are informed that in Saginaw a petition for Mr. Sanborn's reappointment has been quite generally signed by businessmen. We also learn that a number of letters favoring Gen. Hartsuff's appointment have been secured and sent to Senator Conger, but we have not heard of a circulation of any general petition in his favor. Gen. Hartsuff, in an interview with a reporter of the Morning Telegraph, *has set forth his die of the question in its strongest light and with moderation. He says that the Michigan delegation in Congress unanimously agreed to support any man for the place who might be presented by Senator Conger, provided that he was a fit candidate. He says furthermore that it has been the custom for many years and in all parties for the Congressional delegation to name the men to be chosen for such offices and he sees no reason why the custom should not be departed from in this case. This introduces a question that has been much discussed for some years past, and has caused the widest difference ever known in the Republican party. Senator Conkling fought for it and was defeated, the only difference being that in that famous contest, the issue was between senatorial dictation and executive independence, while in this case, it is or may be, between senatorial dictation and executive preferences of the people.*

Rumors began to circulate that Sanborn was going to retire and that the Michigan delegation supported Hartsuff's appointment. A report in the *Port Huron Daily Times* on December 8, 1882, stated:

Mr. Sanborn is a candidate for reappointment with Senator Conger's assurance that he (Conger) holds the matter within his own control and will give due consideration to the wishes of the people of the district. It will thus be seen that Gen. Hartsuff is quite certain of the appointment unless Mr. Sanborn succeeds in convincing Senator Conger through memorials from the people of the district, that such an appointment would be unpopular and unwise. This Mr. Sanborn will no doubt endeavor to do.

While the contest continued between Hartsuff and Sanborn, Senator Ferry also had a fight on his hands. His seat in Congress was set to expire, and he was working hard to muster up the vote of the members of the Michigan Legislature to maintain his seat. He had been serving as a Michigan U.S. Senator since 1871. Unknown to Ferry, his unraveling had already been set in motion in early November. According to a letter to Thomas W. Palmer from his business associate J.B. Whittier of Detroit on November 5, 1882, a scheme was developing among members of the Michigan Republican Party to unseat Ferry and run a new man in his place. Whittier disclosed that thirty officeholders had met in secret to persuade Ferry opponents to boycott Ferry's caucus in the new year. Palmer, who had political aspirations and had failed in 1880 to garner the Republican nomination for Governor of Michigan, had interest in the Ferry seat.

On December 11, 1882, a special report in the *New York Tribune* on the Ferry fight was reprinted in the *Port Huron Daily Times*:

> *It appears that there is a very strong undercurrent of opposition to Mr. Ferry throughout the state and that Congressmen begin to realize that he will find it irresistible. Among things mentioned as causes of the opposition is Senator Ferry's alleged bossism. They assert that during the recent campaign Federal office holders under pay, who owe their offices to Mr. Ferry's influence were engaged in traveling about the state in his interest; and other grave accusations of a political nature were brought against him. It is assured moreover that no love is lost between Senator Ferry and his colleagues, some of whose friends think they have reason to believe that Mr. Ferry has sought to punish them for the part they took in securing Mr. Conger's election to the senate.*

On the same day, it was reported that Conger gave this response when questioned about Senator Ferry: "Mr. Conger when approached today did not care to be interviewed about that portion of the article which relates to him. He says that he has had no hand whatever in the senatorial fight. Members of the legislature were elected, and it is their duty and privilege to elect a senator. He had said or done nothing in connection with the question and does not think he is called upon to meddle in the matter."

Initially, St. Clair County Republicans J.P. Sanborn, Fred Wells, Henry Howard and William Hartsuff were Ferry supporters. The St. Clair County Michigan Legislative Representatives who would be voting on the Ferry seat were composed of representatives with different party affiliations. There was Henry Meyer, Republican; Byron Parks, Republican; Edward Vincent, Greenback; and Justin Rice Whiting, Greenback. Of these men, Meyer and Vincent were Ferry supporters. However, after Hartsuff was said to have the support of Ferry and Conger for the customhouse appointment, rumors that members of the St. Clair County group were scheming against Ferry in support of Palmer were brought forward by Michigan U.S. House Representative John T. Rich on January 6, 1883, in the *Port Huron Daily Times*:

> *Representative Rich was asked today for his opinion about the scheme talked of at Lansing looking to a combination which would send a western man to the Senate and give Detroit Mr. Conger's place four years hence. Mr. Rich said that he had heard the matter talked of when in Michigan and believed that there were a great many St. Clair County people in the movement. The fight over the collectorship of customs at Port Huron, Mr. Rich thinks is the reason for the feeling by St. Clair people. Mr. Rich is not very anxious to see Gen. Hartsuff appointed although he signed his paper when it was first brought forward.*

John T. Rich was the man who won Omar Conger's U.S. House seat after he vacated it to join the U.S. Senate, and he was a member of the same local congressional caucus as the St. Clair County men. His statement alludes to the fact there was a rift forming between the St. Clair County Republicans and that, perhaps, Sanborn was using the support of his cousin Palmer as leverage to threaten Conger to tread cautiously on the Hartsuff appointment through Rich. The scheme to unseat Ferry was reported the same day. While the balloting was not to take place until January 16 in Lansing, it was reported that some Republican men would make the stand against Ferry and that without their vote, he could not be elected. These men were known as the anti-Ferry caucus, and they numbered about twenty-one. On January 8, 1883, it was reported that because Hartsuff had campaigned for Ferry's reelection, several U.S. House representatives who had initially recommended his application for the customhouse appointment were withdrawing their names for him. They explained they had signed the application only because past practice dictated the appointment to Senator Conger.

On January 8, 1883, it was also rumored that it was not the St. Clair County men scheming for Conger's seat; instead, it was Ferry. It was reported that Ferry and his supporters had made a bargain with the Detroit men that if they voted for Ferry, he would aid them in defeating Conger in 1886 and help elect a Detroit man to the seat. Defending the St. Clair County men, the *Port Huron Daily Times* reported on January 8, 1883:

As to St. Clair County men being in it, we have strong doubts. Gen. Hartsuff as Conger's next friend could not be suspected of it, although he may have known that such a bargain was made; and we have not been able to obtain any proof whatever that any prominent Republicans of St. Clair County except the General and his friends, are at all anxious to see Mr. Ferry re-elected or are at work on his behalf. At all events there is not love lost enough for Detroit politicians among Port Huron Republicans to admit the possibility of their entering into a contract to help one of them into Mr. Conger's place.

On January 9, 1883, in a personal letter, Thomas Palmer disclosed to his friend Sam H. Row that he could be used as a compromise candidate in the event Ferry was not reelected. Palmer had been advised to continue to show his support for Ferry in public. But Ferry and his men would have been privy to the whisperings of Palmer's people. The fact that he tried to negotiate with the Detroit men is evidence Ferry knew about this. On January 16, 1883, when the Michigan Legislature met to hold balloting, Ferry received only fifty-nine votes. Byron G. Stout received fifty. Stout was the candidate for the fusionist vote, which was made up of both Democrats and Greenbacks. On the same day the legislature met to vote, a critique of the new civil service reform bill, which, by that time, had been passed by both congressional houses and signed by the President, was reported in the *Port Huron Daily Times*: "Although the real essence of the civil service reform bill is that it seeks to divorce politics from patronage and emphatically declares that no recommendation by a senator or representative of any candidate for office shall even be considered by the appointing power, yet representatives have already been pestered with applications for appointments as members of the commission created by the bill."

Rumors were also circulating that some of Ferry's supporters would favor U.S. House Representative Lacey from Michigan as a possible second candidate if Ferry could not win reelection. It was reported that Conger would favor Lacey's appointment, as he was from the central portion of the state and his location would not interfere with Conger's chances for reelection in 1886. The Michigan Legislature continued to vote each day it was in session until a candidate won. By late January, Palmer men were on the ground in Lansing trying to drum up votes for him, and Henry Howard from Port Huron was in Lansing trying to work for Ferry votes. Also in late January, Michigan House Representative Meyer from the St. Clair County District decided to pull his vote from Ferry. This reduced Ferry's vote to fifty-three.

As Ferry lost favor in Michigan, Hartsuff worried his customhouse appointment was in jeopardy. On January 24, 1883, he went to Washington to salvage his appointment. The *Port Huron Daily Times* reported on the matter:

Gen. Hartsuff of Port Huron, Michigan suddenly turned up here this morning. His object is to look after his candidacy for the Port Huron collectorship and keep the Michigan delegation in line for him, if possible. He is reticent on the senatorial fight, but it is evident he has no hope of Ferry's election. The anti-Hartsuff men in the delegation speak favorably of Edgar Weeks. There is also talk of Rich himself as a compromise candidate for the collectorship. Gen. Hartsuff's chances for being appointed are not nearly so bright as they were some time ago. So far as Senator Conger is concerned it is all plain sailing; he wants Mr. Hartsuff appointed when Mr. Sanborn's term expires and says so, but he is no doubt greatly annoyed and surprised at the opposition which the contemplated appointment has aroused. The matter is to be left to Mr. Conger and Mr. Rich and an effort will be made to compromise without ill feeling.

On January 27, 1883, it was reported that Rich supported Sanborn for the appointment, and the other Ferry vote from the St. Clair County Representative in the Michigan Legislature, Vincent, had been lost. The other anti-Ferry men were said to be willing to compromise on a new candidate if the person was not closely identified with Ferry. The Ferry vote stood at forty. Rumors started circulating the Ferry camp was going after the fusionist vote, and Judge Cooley was mentioned as a Ferry replacement. Hartsuff, who was not getting the confirmation he needed in Washington, was reportedly frustrated on January 27, 1883, as reported by the *Port Huron Daily Times*: "Gen. Hartsuff says the trouble with the Republican party is that the bloody shirt is gone. It has been waved and washed until not a sanguinary tint or single thread remains. There is no other issue around which the party can rally and every man from alderman up is ambitious to go higher, even into the White House, causing any amount of contention and knifing within the organization."

By January 31, 1883, it was reported that Hartsuff had been sent home by Senator Conger and asked to win back the friendship of his fellow U.S. House Representatives from Michigan, Horr, Burrows, Webber, Willits and Rich. These representatives had not been willing to meet with Hartsuff on the matter and were not interested in being bulldozed or converted. They all considered Hartsuff's backing of Ferry for the senatorial contest as a blunder, and his appointment hinged on the outcome of the senatorial race. Rich was reported as saying that the party was against the appointment of Hartsuff and Sanborn at that point. His thinking was that the party desired the appointment of a new man, but on behalf of Senator Conger, they would allow him to name the appointment. Rich hoped Conger would choose a new man. He brought up civil service reform as the reasoning behind his change of heart and that of his Washington colleagues.

By early February, there was still no break in the Ferry vote in Lansing. Ferry maintained forty-nine votes, with Stout at forty-five. A delegation from Port Huron came with Sanborn to Washington to urge his reappointment as collector. His party consisted of Charles Harrington, William F. Botsford, Frank and Charles Moore, A.R. Avery, Jacob Batchelor of Saginaw and Calvin Blood of Marine City. They visited Senator Conger and made their plea for Sanborn. Conger told the party he had not committed himself to an appointment yet. All the local papers in St. Clair County were busily reporting on the Washington visit, all advocating for Sanborn. The *Detroit Evening News*, as reported in the *Port Huron Daily Times* on February 7, 1883, stated:

> *The Port Huron district is still more alarmed. Sanborn has been collector there since the time of Lincoln and has done able service for his masters. His genius kept the Democrats so divided that they never could find a man to beat Conger for Congress. For twelve long years Sanborn regularly turned Mr. Conger to the House and in return dominated the Huron Peninsula like an autocrat. In a lucky moment Conger slipped into the senate by the treason of a Detroit legislator, and instead of being Sanborn's creature became his master. The finest exercise of authority is the contemplated removal of Sanborn from the custom house. Men who have attained greatness very often resent the services of those who made them. The successor chosen; Gen. Hartsuff does not seem to please everybody in the district. He is as venerable, a barnacle as Mr. Sanborn himself. He has been postmaster of Port Huron ever since the war and many think that he as well as Sanborn has been attached long enough and should be scraped off. Those that think so are the friends of John T. Rich of Lapeer.*

While there may be some truth to this reporting that Conger was Sanborn's man at that time, it is also evident this reporter did not have the historical knowledge of local politics going back to the late 1850s, nor was he apprised of Conger's past legislative meanderings and involvement with

PORT HURON & GRATIOT

Street Railway.

A Car leaves Pine and Military Streets every thirty minutes to connect with all trains east and west on the Grand Trunk Railway.

GENERAL TICKET OFFICE,

NO. 48, HURON AVENUE.

Tickets sold to all points East, West, North, and South Street Car Fare 10 cents by day 25 cents by night. Baggage extra. A Baggage Wagon runs in connection which collects and delivers baggage about the City Free of charge

WM. WASTELL,
President.

WM. P. EDISON,
Superintendent.

A Port Huron and Gratiot Street Railway advertisement, as illustrated in the *Brown's City Directory of Port Huron, Michigan*, 1870. *Courtesy of the St. Clair County Public Library.*

major Republicans from the state since the inception of the Republican Party. Conger, James W. Sanborn and Zachariah Chandler were closely connected, and it wasn't until after their deaths in 1870 and 1879 that J.P. Sanborn gained his political clout in the area. By that time, Conger had been involved in politics for almost twenty-three years, and during most of that time, Sanborn was not a major political player. This reporter seems to attribute James W. Sanborn's power to J.P over time and assumes Conger was in debt to him. This was simply untrue; Conger owed no debt to J.P. Sanborn. In truth, the Detroit men had it out for Conger since he won his election to the senate, when their favored candidate, John J. Bagley, was ousted by a vote of Adam Bloom. Adam Bloom had been talked into voting for Conger by Hartsuff.

In the end, Sanborn and Ferry both lost out. Hartsuff obtained the appointment, and Ferry lost to Thomas Palmer on the eighty-third vote.

Being that Palmer was a representative of Detroit, Conger lost his seat in 1887, as Michigan did not like having two senators from the same area. It was reported that Conger tried to make up with Sanborn at the Republican Presidential Convention in 1884, but Sanborn was unwilling to accept his apology. These two controversies serve to illustrate how the factional fight within the Republican Party at the time affected circumstances on a state and local level in Michigan and how Conger ended up eventually losing his seat. This fight led the party to lose the national election in 1884 to Democrat Grover Cleveland, and it lost its foothold in the U.S. Senate and House for the first time since 1860.

THE EDISON CONTROVERSY

The customhouse controversy was not J.P. Sanborn's first controversial go around in Port Huron. In fact, after his uncle's death in 1870, J.P. Sanborn inserted himself into another situation to show his fellow Port Huronites he was a man to be reckoned with locally. In 1865, Port Huron's chief business consisted of the handling of pine logs, which floated down Black River to the lumber mills. The lumber would then travel by railcar to various locations. The station for the Grand Trunk Railroad was located on the northeast corner of the military reservation on the St. Clair River, a short distance south of State Street and east of Fort Gratiot. Butler Street was a main business street at the time, and a ferry used to take passengers from Butler Street to the station.

William Pitt Edison, the older brother of Thomas Alva Edison, owned and operated a horse stable on the west side of Huron Avenue at the time. He came up with the idea to develop a horse-drawn line to take people back and forth from the station. He talked the idea over with William Wastell, who was a young druggist in town and the husband of Martin Gillett's only daughter, Ann. William was interested in the idea. On October 9, 1865, the manager of the Grand Trunk shops, Gage M. Cooper; William Wastell; and William Pitt Edison petitioned the common council for a right-of-way on the reservation for the Port Huron and Gratiot Street Railway Company. The measure did not pass the first time it was presented. At a special meeting of the common council, held on November 21, another ordinance was introduced and passed. The ordinance called for the laying of a single or double track railway from the north end of Huron Avenue, south across

Black River Bridge, to the north line of Pine Street with a fare of ten cents. However, to be able to build over the military reservation area, the company needed the approval of the federal government. A joint resolution was passed in the U.S. House and Senate on January 25, 1866, and signed five days later by President Johnson. The resolution authorized the use of the reservation for a horse-drawn line from Port Huron to the depot. The road was formally opened on October 8, 1866.

The stockholders of the company at the time were William Pitt Edison, William Wastell, John Hibbard, Gage M. Cooper, James Moffatt, John Miller and Gurdon Williams. The road was profitable, and business ran well. In January the following year, the company opened an office and waiting room by the Huron House on the west side of Huron Avenue. Eventually, the company decided to run a night car for passengers arriving on the late train. It commissioned the common council on March 18, 1867, for its approval to raise the night rate to twenty-five cents starting after 8:00 p.m. A resolution was passed. Shortly thereafter, there was an incident involving the night fare rate. D.B. Harrington, who was getting off a late train, refused to pay more than ten cents for his fare. William Pitt Edison made Harrington get out of the car after he refused to pay the night rate fare. In retaliation, D.B. Harrington had William Pitt Edison arrested. Edison was tried in federal court in May 1867, because the depot was located on federal property. The court sided with Edison and justified the higher fare. Trouble seemed to brew for William Pitt Edison from there.

By 1870, the shareholders in the company were John Miller, William Wastell, Gage Cooper, William Stewart, William Hartsuff and William Pitt Edison. Holding only thirty shares, William Pitt. decided it might be a good idea to start retaining a greater portion of stock in the company. He bought out the Cooper and Miller stock. William Hartsuff sold his stock to William Wastell, Thomas Fogg and P.S. Stephenson. In 1872, Wastell and William Pitt had a falling out, whereas Wastell promptly left the company, taking Fogg and Stewart with him.

In March 1873, James Beard, J.H. White, John P. Sanborn, J.F. Batchelor, Larned Smith, William Wastell and John Hibbard formed the Fourth Street and Lapeer Avenue Street Railway to compete against William Pitt Edison's railway. Nothing was done with their new company, and in June of the same year, John Cole, William Hartsuff, Asa Larned, D.B. Harrington, James Beard, F.H. Vanderburgh, John P. Sanborn, W.D. Wright, Oscar A. Wilson and E.S. Petit formed the City Railroad Company and petitioned the common council for permission to construct a street railway. Also during this time, the Grand Trunk had moved the site of its passenger station, leaving a small distance of land between the Edison railway track and the depot. Collector of Customs J.P. Sanborn used this opportunity to exert his influence over Grand Trunk, causing it to issue an injunction against the Edison railway, citing that the street railway company could no longer operate within its railyards.

This action forced the Edison railway to go to the federal government to review the matter. The U.S. Attorney General investigated the rights of the railroad and found that the street railway had no right to cross the railroad's lands without the railroad's consent. This competitive war between the two companies prompted Omar Conger to get involved and work out an arrangement for the Edison railway to resume business.

In 1874, James Beard reassigned ten shares of his stock in the Edison railway to William Wastell. In turn, Wastell and others filed suit against the company, charging that Edison had collaborated with other stockholders to hold a majority of stock and prevented minority shareholders from knowing the business of the railway. In the suit, Wastell was accused of trying to reduce the Edison railway's income by using his influence to get the Grand Trunk Depot office to stop selling Edison railway tickets and sell only the tickets of the City Railroad Company.

A postcard of the Masonic home, East San Gabriel, California, circa 1907. *Author's image.*

Competition between the two companies continued to smolder until 1877, when they merged to form the Port Huron Railway Company. This time, Thomas Edison stepped in and became the primary stockholder of the company to protect his brother from Sanborn and Wastell. The company was formed by Thomas Edison, William Wastell, William Stewart, James Beard, James Goulden, John P. Sanborn, John Cole, Isaac Linsbury, O'Brien J. Atkinson, A.E. Chadwick, Lucian Howe and George P. Voorheis. When William Pitt retired from the company, Thomas Edison sold his shares, too. John P. Sanborn took over the Wastell and Edison shares and eventually sold the company in 1886 to the Talbot brothers, who turned it into an electric streetcar system.

THE SANBORN FAMILY CONTROVERSY

After J.P. Sanborn left the customhouse, he decided to focus on business opportunities in California. In the summer of 1887, he filed for partnership with H.H. Markham, L.W. Dennis, Nelson Vanderslip and C.H. Bradley in a company called the Pacific Water Company. The company was located in southern California. The company was organized to develop a water system in the San Gabriel Valley. By 1890, J.P. and his brother James M. Sanborn and their families all moved from Port Huron to San Gabriel. The company built a grand hotel there called Hotel San Gabriel. John P. Sanborn, his wife, his brother and his son made frequent visits to the hotel. The hotel was later known as the Masonic Home after it was purchased by the Masons of Southern California to be used as a shelter for aged and infirmed Masons in 1907.

At the same time J.P. entered business with the Pacific Water Company in 1887, he also purchased two thousand acres of land in partnership with Simon Murphy, a wealthy Detroit lumberman; James W. Sanborn's widow, Mehitable Sanborn; and his oldest son, Fred Sanborn, in Ramirez, California. The land was full of fruit trees. They planned on developing the land into a town called East Whittier. After 1890, things turned sour between J.P. and James Sanborn's family. They also turned sour with his partners in the Pacific Water Company. J.P. found himself in court with both parties. In August 1890, J.P. and his business associates of the Pacific Water Company were in court over a suit concerning the company's stock. The litigation continued until 1894, when J.P. lost his stock in the company.

In 1891, as an heir to the James W. Sanborn estate, Fred Sanborn filed suit against J.P., alleging that while acting as the trustee of his father's estate, he had mismanaged estate funds, resulting in the squandering of his inheritance. He accused J.P. of using estate funds to make his own personal purchases. When James W. Sanborn died in 1870, he left three children, Nancy, Fred and William Sanborn. Nancy was an adult, as she was the child of his first wife. Fred and William were minors and children of his third wife, Mehitable. James W. Sanborn's will called for oversight of his estate until his youngest son, William, reached the age of adulthood. William, an incompetent person, turned eighteen in 1891, at which time, the estate proceeds were to have been divided between James's children, William, Fred and Nancy. By 1891, Nancy was deceased, leaving two small children and a husband, William F. Botsford. During the litigation proceedings, Mehitable was appointed guardian over her son William, and William Botsford was appointed guardian over his two children.

After Fred Sanborn filed suit in 1891, J.P agreed to step down as trustee and assign the assets of the estate to Fred. However, it was soon discovered that J.P. had not filed an annual account on the estate since the death of his co-trustee, Newell Avery, in 1878. Documentation showed the estate was valued at $212,997.12 at the time of James Sanborn's death in 1870. J.P. could not produce competent records of his management of the funds and was ordered to deliver a statement to Fred Sanborn after filing a generalized statement with the court on March 6, 1891. In Fred Sanborn's petition to the court, he asked that John P. Sanborn be cited for his failure to file an account and keeping the books of the James Sanborn estate hidden from him. His petition was dated October 17, 1891, in which he stated:

> On or about the 6th day of March, 1891, the said Sanborn filed in said Probate Court a statement in which he admitted that there was in his possession as executor of said estate, $123,954.50 of the personal property and a large amount of real estate, but that said statement does not contain a full and complete list of the assets as your petitioner verily believes, and that it is impossible to ascertain from said statement what the character of the assets of said estate may be and whether the same are good or bad or of any value whatever, or whether they are in fact any assets in the hands of said Sanborn as such executor and that the statement filed by said Sanborn is not such as he was in duty bound and required to file, and is so incomplete, uncertain and insufficient, that it is in fact no statement of account whatever and should be disregarded as absolutely worthless and of

no effect in enabling the Court to determine what assets said Sanborn has or had in possession belonging to the estate.

Being ordered to file an account, J.P. Sanborn produced a statement showing the estate was valued at only $24,271.61. In his answer to Fred Sanborn's petition, J.P. stated that he had built a home for the family that cost $35,000, paid James's widow for support, paid Nancy Sanborn for support, gave the family loans, that he had purchased them buildings, et cetera, over the course of his representation of the estate. In all, he stated that he had given roughly $207,334 directly to the Sanborn family. He also defended himself against Fred Sanborn's claims that he had purposefully kept James W. Sanborn's estate books from him. In his answer, J.P. stated:

The respondent denies that there were any books of the estate of James W. Sanborn in his possession, but he insists that the only books in his possession were his own private books; he denied that the offices kept by him was the office of James W. Sanborn & Company, but insists that the same was the office of this respondent in which he carried on not only the business entrusted to him as executor and trustee of the estate of James W. Sanborn, but that he also carried on the business in said office of the trustee of the estate of Mary Jane Sweetser, deceased, also the business of James W. Sanborn & Company, but he also at the said office was known by the name of the office of James W. Sanborn & Company, but he also at said place carried on the business of A & D Rust, Sanborn Rust & Company, Abner Coburn, Avery & Murphy, and Gerrish, Murphy & Company of the Avery heirs and to some extent the business of himself, and that the books and accounts there were in the said James W. Sanborn & Company offices were the books of this respondent, and not of the said estate of James W. Sanborn.

As the parties began litigating the case, it was discovered that J.P. Sanborn had used estate funds to pay for his investment in the Port Huron and Northwestern Railroad in 1878, the purchase of his home on Seventh Street, an investment in the Chicago and Lake Huron Railroad and the construction of the Sanborn Block on Water Street. The litigation continued for years. In 1898, J.P. Sanborn entered into a settlement agreement with the James W. Sanborn children, in which he turned over the title of his home on Seventh Street to them and gave them a cash settlement of over $16,000. Fred Sanborn became trustee of the estate and managed its interest going forward.

St. Joseph Catholic Church, 2023, the former site of the John P. Sanborn home. *Author's image.*

In 1906, J.P.'s home was leased to the Port Huron Board of Education to be used as a temporary high school. In 1912, Fred sold both the Sanborn homes on Seventh Street on behalf of the estate. The family moved to Los Angeles in 1913. J.P. and his family continued living in the Los Angeles area. The Mehitabel Sanborn home still stands on Seventh Street, while the J.P. Sanborn homestead now holds the St. Joseph Catholic Church. After J.P.'s death in 1914, the *Port Huron Daily Times* reported that he had lost his fortune in California to litigation and land speculation ventures in Whitter, California. And while he had spent his final years in poverty, J.P. never lost his old fighting spirit. It reported, "If there was any regret for the passing of the days when he entertained notables and men sought him for the power and influence, he wielded, he never expressed it, but kept on at his daily tasks until illness compelled him to quit."

Whether he ever admitted to it or not, J.P. Sanborn's controversial nature led him to lose more than just money over his lifetime. Severing ties with Omar Conger and the children of his beloved uncle James W. Sanborn had to have made quite an impact.

BIBLIOGRAPHY

Chapter 1

Ancestry. "A Biographical Sketch of Elkanah Watson." North American Family Histories 1500–2000. 2016. https://www.ancestry.com/discoveryui-content/view/3339496:61157.

———. "Charlotte Sanborn Estate File, Cal. 1, No. 511, *Probate Calendars and Estate Files, 1828–1902; Probate Index, 1838–1975;* Author*: Michigan. Probate Court (St. Clair County);* Probate Place*: St Clair, Michigan."* Michigan, U.S., *Wills and Probate Records, 1784–1980* [database on-line]. 2015. https://www.ancestry.com/discoveryui-content/view/359498:8793?_phsrc=FfJ844&_phstart=successSource&gsfn=charlotte&gsln=sanborn&ml_rpos=1&queryId=2452dd2dd53bece32265db3031504f76.

———. "James Sanborn Estate File, Cal 2, No. 498, Cal. 2, No. 527 and Cal. 4, No. 9, *Probate Calendars and Estate Files, 1828–1902; Probate Index, 1838–1975*; Author*: Michigan. Probate Court (St. Clair County)*; Probate Place: *St Clair, Michigan."* Michigan, U.S., *Wills and Probate Records, 1784–1980* [database on-line]. 2015. https://www.ancestry.com/discoveryui-content/view/292214:8793?_phsrc=FfJ849&_phstart=successSource&gsfn=james&gsln=sanborn&ml_rpos=3&queryId=14b0a4863dab7a664b57f887e2302fd1.

———. "Martin S. Gillett Estate File, Cal. 2, No. 213, *Probate Calendars and Estate Files, 1828–1902; Probate Index, 1838–1975*; Author*: Michigan. Probate Court (St. Clair County);* Probate Place*: St Clair, Michigan, Michigan,*

U.S., Wills and Probate Records, 1784-1980 [database on-line]. 2015. https://www.ancestry.com/discoveryui-content/view/244535:8793?_phsrc=FfJ853&_phstart=successSource&gsfn=martin&gsln=gillett&ml_rpos=1&queryId=4e72191bc6123dff0b45b194f44299c3.

———. "Mary J. Sweetser Estate File, Cal. 2, No. 5552, *Probate Calendars and Estate Files, 1828–1902; Probate Index, 1838–1975;* Author*: Michigan. Probate Court (St. Clair County)*; Probate Place: *St Clair, Michigan."* *Michigan, U.S., Wills and Probate Records, 1784–1980* [database on-line]. 2015. https://www.ancestry.com/discoveryui-content/view/244063:8793?_phsrc=FfJ851&_phstart=successSource&gsfn=mary&gsln=sweetser&ml_rpos=1&queryId=7f6eab88c7e2559e9e51508ffde09c67.

Andreas, A.T. *History of St. Clair County, Michigan.* Chicago, IL: A.T. Andreas and Co., 1883.

Benevolent and Protective Order of the Elks of the United States of America. "National and Local Lodge 343 History, Port Huron, Michigan." https://www.elks.org/lodges/NewsStory.cfm?StoryID=125860&LodgeNumber=343.

Blue Water Chamber of Commerce. "The Chamber Area." https://www.bluewaterchamber.com/chamber-area.html#:~:text=Sixty%20miles%20north%20of%20Detroit,of%20Lake%20Huron%2C%20the%20St.

Bureau of Land Management. "Michigan Territory: Withdrawal of Lands Adjacent to St. Clair River for Military Purposes, Executive Order of President John Quincy Adams. November 11, 1828. Accession No. 1828-41-1. Record group 49. National Archives and Records Administration." Proquest Congressional Database. https://congressional.proquest.com/congressional.

Burton, Clarence M. *Governor and Judges Journal: Proceedings of the Land Board of Detroit.* Edited by Agnew M. Burton. Detroit: Michigan Commission on Land Titles, 1915. Google Books. https://www.google.com/books/edition/Governor_and_Judges_Journal/AzkVAAAAYAAJ?hl=en&gbpv=0.

Canadian Encyclopedia. "Sombra Township Treaty (No. 7)." https://www.thecanadianencyclopedia.ca/en/article/sombra-township-treaty-no-7.

Carter, Clarence E., ed. *The Territorial Papers of the United States.* Vol. 10. *The Territory of Michigan 1805–1820.* Washington, D.C.: Government Printing Office, 1942. Google Books. https://www.google.com/books/edition/The_Territorial_Papers_of_the_United_Sta/alRNofg-PbMC?hl=en&gbpv=1.

Detroit Free Press. Merchants' Exchange Block Rental advertisement. October 22, 1855. www.newspapers.com.

Detroit Gazette. Marriage announcement of Michael Kerley and Margaret Berthelet. "Vital Records from the Detroit Gazette 1817–1830." Collected by Beulah Puffer Kresge. *Detroit Society for Genealogical Research Magazine* 5, no. 6 (March 1942): 113–14.

Devito, Lee. "Boutique Hotel with Floating Barge Bar Opening in Port Huron in Nearly 100-Year-Old-Bank." *Detroit Metro Times*, May 12, 2022. https://www.metrotimes.com/food-drink/boutique-hotel-with-floating-barge-bar-opening-in-port-huron-in-nearly-100-year-old-former-bank-30033847.

Durfee, Eleazer D., and D. Gregory Sanford. "A Guide to the Henry Stevens Collection at the Vermont State Archives." Vermont State Archives. https://sos.vermont.gov/media/e0tbs5x3/stevens_collection.pdf.

1818 Michigan Original Survey. Fractional Township West of St. Clair River, Township 6 N Range 17E, DM No. 27365 [illustration]. U.S. Department of the Interior, Bureau of Land Management. https://glorecords.blm.gov/details/survey/default.aspx?dm_id=27366&sid=ue2rkddj.gcc#surveyDetailsTabIndex=0.

Family Search. "Deed from Alvah Sweetser and J.W. Sanborn to Martin S. Gillett, July 18, 1851, St. Clair County, Michigan Land Records 1821–1927; index 1821–1901, Deed Records v. R–S 1849–1851, Liber S, Pages 631, 632 (693, 694 of 784 pages of film)." https://www.familysearch.org/search/catalog/244706?availability=Family%20History%20Library.

———. "Deed from Charlotte Sanborn to Alvah Sweetser and J.W. Sanborn, July 18, 1854, St. Clair County, Michigan Land Records 1821–1927; index 1821–1901, Deed Records v. X–Y 1854–1855, Liber X, Page 134 (74 of 704 pages of film)." https://www.familysearch.org/search/catalog/244706?availability=Family%20History%20Library.

———. "Deed from Cummings Sanborn to Fortune White, June 25, 1849, St. Clair County, Michigan Land Records 1821–1927; index 1821–1901, Deed Records v. P–Q 1847–1849, Liber Q, Page 632 (671 of 677 pages of film)." https://www.familysearch.org/search/catalog/244706?availability=Family%20History%20Library.

———. "Deed from E.L. Hannah to Peter Brakeman, April 10, 1837, St. Clair County, Michigan Land Records 1821–1927; index 1821–1901, Deed and Mortgage Records v. E & F 1835–1838, Liber F, Pages 217–219 (393, 394 of 585 pages of film)." https://www.familysearch.org/search/catalog/244706?availability=Family%20History%20Library.

————. "Deed from Fortune White to Alvah Sweetser and J.W. Sanborn, June 15, 1849, St. Clair County, Michigan Land Records 1821–1927; index 1821–1901, Deed Records v. R–S 1849–1851, Liber R, Page 2 (7 of 784 pages of film)." https://www.familysearch.org/search/catalog/244706?availability=Family%20History%20Library.

————. "Deed from John H. Westbrook to Martin S. Gillett, March 21, 1843, St. Clair County, Michigan Land Records 1821–1927; index 1821–1901, Deed Index v. 1–4 1821–1868, Liber M, Page 129 (Liber missing from collection, only index available) (280 of 792 pages of film)." https://www.familysearch.org/search/catalog/244706?availability=Family%20History%20Library.

————. "Deed from John H. Westbrook to S.V. Thornton, May 4, 1837, St. Clair County, Michigan Land Records 1821–1927; index 1821–1901, Deed and Mortgage Records v. G and H 1837–1838,18–19 (321 of 606 pages of film)." https://www.familysearch.org/search/catalog/244706?availability=Family%20History%20Library.

————. "Deed from Joseph and Ann Watson to D.B. Harrington, July 24, 1835, St. Clair County, Michigan Land Records 1821–1927; index 1821–1901, Deed and Mortgage Records v. B, C, D 1830–1837, Liber No. 3, Page 120 (379, 380 of 791 pages of film)." https://www.familysearch.org/search/catalog/244706?availability=Family%20History%20Library.

————. "Deed from Joseph Watson to Michael L. Kerley, March 27, 1835, St. Clair County, Michigan Land Records 1821–1927; index 1821–1901, Transcription No. 1 for v. C–E 1833 to 1836, Transcription No. 1, Page 189 (112, 113 of 317 pages of film)." https://www.familysearch.org/search/catalog/244706?availability=Family%20History%20Library.

————. "Deed from J.P. Sanborn, Trustee to Henry McMorran, December 23, 1892, St. Clair County, Michigan Land Records 1821–1927; index 1821–1901, Deed Records v. 68–69 1880–1881, Liber 69, Page 556 (608 of 613 pages of film)." https://www.familysearch.org/search/catalog/244706?availability=Family%20History%20Library.

————. "Deed from Michel L. Kerley to Elihu L. Hannah and Stephen V. Thornton, December 2, 1835, St. Clair County, Michigan Land Records 1821–1927, index 1821–1901, Transcription No. 1 for v. C–E 1833 to 1836, Transcription No. 1, Page 191, (113 of 317 pages of film)." https://www.familysearch.org/search/catalog/244706?availability=Family%20History%20Library.

————. "Deed from P.F. Brakeman to John H. Westbrook, April 20, 1837, St. Clair County, Michigan Land Records 1821–1927; index 1821–1901, Deed and Mortgage Records v. E and F 1835–1838, Liber F, Pages 219–220 (394 of 585 pages of film)." https://www.familysearch.org/search/catalog/244706?availability=Family%20History%20Library.

————. "Deed from Stephen V. Thornton to Cummings Sanborn, February 19, 1846, St. Clair County, Michigan Land Records 1821–1927; index 1821–1901, Deed Records v. R–S 1849–1851, Liber S, Page 89 (419 of 784 pages of film)." https://www.familysearch.org/search/catalog/244706?availability=Family%20History%20Library.

————. "Deed from Stephen V. Thornton to John H. Westbrook, May 4, 1837, St. Clair County, Michigan Land Records 1821–1927; index 1821–1901, Deed and Mortgage Records v. G and H 1837–1838, Liber G, Pages 112–113 (91, 92 of 606 pages of film)." https://www.familysearch.org/search/catalog/244706?availability=Family%20History%20Library.

————. "Letter from Henry R. Schoolcraft to John Hulbert, January 15, 1840, Records of the Michigan Superintendency of Indian Affairs, 1814–1851: NARA RG 75 Publication, MI, Letters Sent v. 2 1839–1842, Manuscript Pages 204–205 (109 of 362 pages of film)." https://www.familysearch.org/search/catalog/589956?availability=Family%20History%20Library.

————. "Letter from Nay-kee-shick to President Martin Van Buren, November 2, 1837, Records of the Michigan Superintendency of Indian Affairs, 1814–1851: NARA RG 75 Publication, MI, Letters Received v. 3 1837 (NARA Series, MI, Roll 43), Manuscript Pages 231–233 (231–233 of 324 pages of film)." https://www.familysearch.org/search/catalog/589956?availability=Family%20History%20Library.

Find a Grave. "Col. Joseph Watson." https://www.findagrave.com/memorial/124275206/joseph-watson.

Fuller, George Newman, PhD. *Economic and Social Beginnings of Michigan: A Study of the Settlement of the Lower Peninsula, During the Territorial Period 1805–1837*. Lansing, MI: Wynkoop Hallenbeck Crawford Co. State Printers, 1916.

Gates, Paul W. *History of Public Land Law Development*. Vol. 62. Washington, D.C.: Public Land Law Review Commission, 1968. Google Books. https://www.google.com/books/edition/History_of_Public_Land_Law_Development/uNe5AAAAIAAJ?hl=en.

Gilman, Robert. "The Idea of Owning Land: An Old Notion by the Sword Is Quietly Undergoing a Profound Transformation." Context Institute. https://www.context.org/iclib/ic08/gilman1/.

Harrington, Daniel B. *Michigan Historical Collections, Report of the Pioneer Society of Michigan.* Vol. 5. Lansing: Michigan Historical Commission, 1905.

Harvard Law School. "*Williams v. Berthelet,* 2 Blume Sup. Ct. Trans. 240, Michigan Supreme Court, September 30, 1808." Caselaw Access Project. https://cite.case.law/blume-sup-ct-trans/2/240/.

Hele, Karl S., ed. "We Have No Spirit to Celebrate with You." In *Lines Drawn Upon the Water: First Nations and the Great Lakes Borders and Borderlands.* Waterloo, CA: Wilfrid Laurier University, 2008.

"Introduction." In *Michigan Historical Collections: Documents Relating to Detroit and Vicinity 1805–1813.* Vol. 40. Lansing: Michigan Historical Commission, 1929.

Jenks, W.L. "Early Port Huron Montgats and Peru." *Port Huron Times Herald,* April 25, 1914. www.newspapers.com.

———. "The First Bank in St. Clair County." In *First National Exchange Bank: Fifty Years of Banking 1871–1921.* Port Huron, MI: Riverside Printing Company, n.d., ca. 1921. https://mdoe.state.mi.us/legislators/BibliographySource?sortOrder=sourcecode_desc&page=22.

———. "Historian Relates Interesting Facts About Pioneer Citizens." *Port Huron Times Herald,* May 28, 1929. www.newspapers.com.

———. "History of Site Recalls Early Days in Port Huron: First Business Dates Back 93 Years Was Indian Reservation Until Government Made New Chippewa Treaty." *Port Huron Times Herald,* August 18, 1928. www.newspapers.com.

———. *St. Clair County, Michigan: Its History and Its People: A Narrative Account of Its Historical Progress and Its Principal Interests.* Vol. 1. New York: Lewis Publishing Company, 1912.

Mariners' Museum and Park: The Ages of Exploration. "Jacques Cartier Explorer Age of Discovery." https://exploration.marinersmuseum.org/subject/jacques-cartier/#:~:text=They%20stopped%20at%20a%20village,reached%20Hochelaga%20(now%20Montr%C3%A9al).

Martin, Geo W., ed. "The Chippewas and Munsee (or Christian) Indians of Franklin County." In *Collections of the Kansas State Historical Society.* Vol. 11. Topeka, KS: State Printing Office, 1910. https://www.google.com/books/edition/Collections_of_the_Kansas_State_Historic/xNBKAQAAMAAJ?q=Esh-ton-o-quot+in+Chippewa,+also+known+as+Mr.+Francis+McCoonse&gbpv=1#f=false.

Michigan House of Representatives. "Townships in Michigan." April 17, 2015. https://www.house.mi.gov/sessiondocs/2015-2016/testimony/Committee339-4-21-2015-1.pdf.

Mitts, Dorothy. "Chapter XXXVI: Municipal Beginnings of Port Huron." *That Noble Country*. Philadelphia, PA: Dorrance and Company, 1969.

———. "Where the Wild Goose Flies: Remembrance of Montgats." *Port Huron Times Herald*. February 22, 1970. http://www.newspapers.com.

National Archives Catalog. "Ratified Indian Treaty 54: Ottawa, Chippewa, Wyandot, and Potawatomi—Detroit, November 7, 1807." https://catalog.archives.gov/id/161303994.

———. "Ratified Indian Treaty 207: Chippewa (Swan Creek and Black River Bands in Michigan)—Washington, D.C., May 9, 1836." https://catalog.archives.gov/id/148026684.

National Park Service. "He Was a Coward." https://www.nps.gov/articles/surrender-of-detroit.htm.

Neumeyer, Elizabeth. "Michigan Indians Battle Against Removal." *Michigan History* 4 (1971): 276–77.

Owens, Jack. "Thomas Smith—Who?—Why?" MSPS Convention. November 23, 2016. https://mispsevents.org/wp-content/uploads/2018/02/Owens-Smith.pdf.

Parker, Phillip. "Court-Martial for Testimony and Release." February 11 and 14, 1814. Joseph Watson Papers, Henry Stevens Collection, 1806–1829. Vermont State Archives.

Plain, David D. *The Plains of Aamjiwnaang: Our History*. Bloomington, IN: Trafford Publishing, 2007.

Port Huron Daily Times. "New Residence for Mrs. J.W. Sanborn." July 14, 1875. www.newspapers.com.

———. "Notice to Patrons of Husbandry." March 28, 1877. www.newspapers.com.

———. "Personal and Society Notes." March 12, 1881. www.newspapers.com.

———. "Pioneer's Death: Mrs. Ann E. Wastell Passed Away at Her Home on Sixth Street: Had Resided in Port Huron for Over Fifty Years: One of the Best Known Women in This Locality." December 14, 1904. www.newspapers.com.

———. "Tonight's Happenings." April 5, 1889. www.newspapers.com.

Port Huron Times Herald. "Bank Building Open, Visited by Thousands: Bankers of State Inspects Structure Entertained at Dinner Friday." August 18, 1928. www.newspapers.com.

———. "Bronze Tablet to Perpetuate Memory of Indian Reservation."
April 3, 1931. http://www.newspapers.com.

———. "D.A.R. Unveils Bronze Tablet: Marker Placed on Site of Indian
Reservation." June 15, 1931. www.newspapers.com.

———. "Early Recollections of Hiram Hamilton: The Aged Mail Carrier
Between Port Huron and Sarnia, People who have Resided in Port
Huron a Half Century." July 19, 1892. www.newspapers.com.

———. "Family Tree of Federal Bank Has Many Branches: History
Revives Traditions of Early Banks Great Names in City's Past Fill
Records of Institution." August 18, 1928. www.newspapers.com.

———. "First National Trust & Savings Bank." September 1, 1936. www.
newspapers.com.

———. "Local Items." December 11, 1893. www.newspapers.com.

———. "Makes Levy on Business Block: Dr. Patrick Seeks to Recover
Debt from John G. Wastell." September 23, 1913. www.newspapers.
com.

———. "Many Changes in Street Since Birth 105 Years Ago." October 9,
1929. www.newspapers.com.

———. "Mrs. Parley Morse." April 5, 1913. www.newspapers.com.

———. "Mrs. Wastell's Will First Provides for Comfort of Her Aged
Mother: Fred W. Wastell Named as Executor without Bonds: At Death
of Mother Entire Estate Goes to Two Sons." December 17, 1904. www.
newspapers.com.

———. "Nothing Left: John G. Wastell Talked About Estate of His
Mother: No Revenue to Support His Aged Grandmother." January 18,
1905. www.newspapers.com.

———. "Old Wastell Block Being Torn Down to Make Way for New Bank
Building, February 14, 1927." www.newspapers.com.

———. "Port Huron Men and Women 90 Years Ago Depicted in Story in
Scrapbook." April 24, 1936. www.newspapers.com.

———. "Port Huron Pioneer Dead: Mrs. Eliza Gillett Passes Away at Age
of 92 Years: Was Prominent in Early Affairs of the Village and City."
March 16, 1912. www.newspapers.com.

———. "Public Auction–Askar Shain Photography Equipment."
November 10, 1990." www.newspapers.com.

———. "Recalls Memories of 70 Years Ago (1861), Fred A. Fish Describes
'Old Timers' Here, Builders of Early Port Huron Live Again in
Retrospect." September 11, 1931. www.newspapers.com.

———. "Sheriff's Sale." October 28, 1913. www.newspapers.com.

———. "Twenty Years Ago Today." May 29, 1914. www.newspapers.com.

Sanborn, V.C. *Genealogy of the Family of Samborne or Sanborn in England and America 1194–1898*. La Grange, IL: Self-published, 1899.

Sewick, Paul. "The Buchanan House Part I: 1750–1895—The Land." Corktown History. March 5, 2011. http://corktownhistory.blogspot.com/2011/03/buchanan-house-part-i-1750-1895-land.html.

Tap, Bruce. "The Evils of Intemperance Are Universally Conceded: The Temperance Debate in Early Grand Rapids." *Michigan Historical Review* 19, no. 1 (Spring 1993): 17–45. https://www.jstor.org/stable/20173371.

Taylor, Hilda A. *First Land Owners of St. Clair County, Michigan*. Lansing: Michigan Genealogical Council, 1978.

TrustConverter. "Cords to Acres Conversion." https://trustconverter.com/en/area-conversion/cords/cords-to-acres.html?value=1.

United States Congress. *American State Papers: Documents, Legislative and Executive of the Congress of the United States in Relation to the Public Lands*. Vol. 4. Washington, D.C.: Duff Green, 1834. https://www.google.com/books/edition/American_State_Papers/chFFAQAAMAAJ?hl=en&gbpv=0.

Watson, Elkanah. "To James Madison from Elkanah Watson, 12 December 1812 (Abstract)." In *The Papers of James Madison*. Presidential Series, vol. 5. *10 July 1812–7 February 1813*. Edited by J.C.A. Stagg, Martha J. King, Ellen J. Barber, Anne Mandeville-Colony, Angela Kreider and Jewel L. Spangler. Charlottesville: University of Virginia Press, 2004. https://founders.archives.gov/documents/Madison/03-05-02-0410.

———. "To James Madison from Elkanah Watson, 25 October 1813." In *The Papers of James Madison*. Presidential Series, vol. 7. *October 25, 1813–June 30, 1814*. Edited by Angela Kreiser, J.C.A. Stagg, Mary Parke Johnson, Anne Mandeville-Colony and Katherine E. Harbury. Charlottesville: University of Virginia Press, 2012. https://founders.archives.gov/documents/Madison/03-07-02-0001.

Watson, Joseph. "To James Madison from Joseph Watson, 11 January 1813 (Abstract)." In *The Papers of James Madison*. Presidential Series, vol. 5. *10 July 1812–7 February 1813*. Edited by J.C.A. Stagg, Martha J. King, Ellen J. Barber, Anne Mandeville-Colony, Angela Kreider and Jewel L. Spangler. Charlottesville: University of Virginia Press, 2004. https://founders.archives.gov/documents/Madison/03-05-02-0480.

Watson, Winslow C., ed. "Letter from Governor Hull to Elkanah Watson, November 30, 1807." In *Men and Times of the Revolution: Memoirs of Elkanah Watson*. New York: Dana and Company, 1856.

Wikipedia. "Elkanah Watson." https://en.wikipedia.org/wiki/Elkanah_Watson.

———. "James Witherell." https://en.wikipedia.org/wiki/James_Witherell.

———. "Macomb County, Michigan." https://en.wikipedia.org/wiki/Macomb_County,_Michigan.

———. "Michigan National Bank." https://en.wikipedia.org/wiki/Michigan_National_Bank.

———. "Michigan Territory." https://en.wikipedia.org/wiki/Michigan_Territory.

———. "Muskrat French." https://en.wikipedia.org/wiki/Muskrat_French.

———. "Port Huron, Michigan." https://en.wikipedia.org/wiki/Port_Huron,_Michigan.

———. "St. Clair County, Michigan." https://en.wikipedia.org/wiki/St._Clair_County,_Michigan.

———. "Thomas W. Palmer." https://en.wikipedia.org/wiki/Thomas_W._Palmer.

———. "War of 1812." https://en.wikipedia.org/wiki/War_of_1812.

Williams, Brenda L. "The First Land Sales in Port Huron." Tapping Roots. https://tappingroots.com/2021/04/03/the-first-land-sales-in-port-huron-michigan/.

Witherell-Palmer, Mary A. "The Wreck of the *Walk-in-the-Water*, Pioneer Steamboat on the Western Lakes, transcribed from the original by Walter Lewis, Halton Hills, ON, Canada: Maritime History of the Great Lakes, 2004." Based on the original document: "The *Wreck of the Walk-in-the-Water*, Pioneer Steamboat on the Western Lakes." *Publications of the Buffalo Historical Society* 5 (January 1902): 319–23. https://www.maritimehistoryofthegreatlakes.ca//documents/walkinthewater/default.asp.

Wyckoff, Larry M. "Michigan's Indian Reservations, 1807–1855." https://www.academia.edu/38816617/Michigans_Indian_Reservations_1807_1855.

Chapter 2

American Biographical History of Eminent and Self Made Men. Vol. 2. *Michigan*. Cincinnati, OH: Western Biographical Publishing Co., 1878. https://quod.lib.umich.edu/m/micounty/bad6019.0002.001/489?q1=american+biographical+history&view=image&size=100.

Andreas, A.T. *History of St. Clair County, Michigan*. Chicago, IL: A.T. Andreas and Co., 1883.

Bailey, Christopher, Tarique Hossain and Gary Pecquet. "Private Banks in Early Michigan, 1837–1884." *Cliometrica; Heidelberg* 12, no. 1 (January 2018): 153–80. https://www.proquest.com/docview/1992977266?pq-or igsite=gscholar&fromopenview=true.

"Biography of Peter W. Reed, M.D., The Seventh Congressional District." In *American Biographical History of Eminent and Self Made Men*. Vol. 2. *Michigan*. Cincinnati, OH: Western Biographical Publishing Co., 1878. https://quod.lib.umich.edu/m/micounty/bad6019.0002.001/489?q1= american+biographical+history&view=image&size=100.

Bromley, Suzette. "Port Huron, Michigan: A Port City Built by the Railroad." Rootsweb. 2005. https://sites.rootsweb.com/~miporthu/ PH_Railroad.htm.

Brown's City Directory of Port Huron, MI of 1871. Port Huron, MI: C. Exera Brown1870. St. Clair County Library. https://stclaircountylibrary.org/ services/list/local_history.

Family Search. "Deed from B.F. Farrand and James Beard, Trustees to Peter W. Reed, January 17, 1878, St. Clair County, Michigan Land Records 1821–1927, index 1821–1901, Deed Records v. 61 1877–1879, Liber 61, Pages 245–246, (129 and 130 of 330 pages of film)." https:// www.familysearch.org/search/catalog/244706?availability=Family%20 History%20Library.

———. "Deed from John Johnston to B.C. Farrand and James Beard, Trustees, May 15, 1877, St. Clair County, Michigan Land Records 1821–1927, index 1821–1901, Deed Records v. 57–58 1876 to 1877, Liber 57, Pages 558–559 (287 and 288 of 655 pages of film)." https:// www.familysearch.org/search/catalog/244706?availability=Family%20 History%20Library.

Federal Reserve History. "Banking Panic of the Gilded Age 1863–1913." https://www.federalreservehistory.org/essays/banking-panics-of-the-gilded-age.

Illustration of John Johnston and Co. and John Miller and Son advertisement. In *Merchant's and Banker's Almanac*. Vol. 32. New York: N.p., 1870. Internet Archive. https://archive.org/details/ merchantsbankers1870newyuoft/mode/2up?q=john+johnston.

Isabell family collection. Photograph of Elizabeth Thacher Reed, circa 1920.

———. Photograph of the Reed house.

———. Photograph of the Robert H. Reed family, circa 1910.

———. Photograph of the sketch of the John Johnston residence. In *Atlas of St. Clair County*. Philadelphia, PA: Everts and Stewart, 1876, 39.

Jarmenski, Matthew. "State Banks and the National Banking Acts: Measuring the Response to Increased Financial Regulation, 1860–1870." *Journal of Money, Credit and Banking* 15, nos. 2–3 (March–April 2013): 379–99. https://www.jstor.org/stable/23463525.

Jenks, W.L. "The First Bank in St. Clair County." In *First National Exchange Bank: Fifty Years of Banking 1871–1921*. Port Huron, MI: Riverside Printing Company, circa 1921. https://mdoe.state.mi.us/legislators/BibliographySource?sortOrder=sourcecode_desc&page=22.

———. *St. Clair County, Michigan: Its History and Its People: A Narrative Account of its Historical Progress and its Principal Interests*. Vol. 1. New York: Lewis Publishing Company, 1912.

Michigan State Medical Society. "Sundry Anecdotes & Brief Biographies, Dr. Peter W. Reed." In *Medical History of Michigan, Michigan State Medical Society*. Vol. 1. Minneapolis, MN: Bruce Publishing Company, 1930. https://www.loc.gov/resource/lhbum.1995a/?sp=456&st=image.

New York Times. "Henry Clews & Co." September 24, 1873. www.newspapers.com.

Port Huron City Directory of 1873. Port Huron, MI: Port Huron Times Company, 1873. St. Clair County Library. https://stclaircountylibrary.org/services/list/local_history.

Port Huron Times. "Brevities: Mr. Bancroft's Report." December 21, 1875. www.newspapers.com.

———. "A Card from Treasurer McMorran." December 27, 1875. www.newspapers.com.

———. "The City Funds." May 7, 1872. www.newspapers.com.

———. "The City Funds." May 23, 1872. www.newspapers.com.

———. "The City Funds." October 13, 1873. www.newspapers.com.

———. "The City Treasury: The Office of Treasurer and the City Funds." March 29, 1875. www.newspapers.com.

———. "Common Council." February 14, 1877. www.newspapers.com.

———. "The County Ticket." September 12, 1872. www.newspapers.com.

———. "The Financial Crisis." September 27, 1873. www.newspapers.com.

———. "From the City Treasurer." March 20, 1877. www.newspapers.com.

———. "Groundless Alarm." December 20, 1875. www.newspapers.com.

———. "John Johnston & Co." August 3, 1874. www.newspapers.com.

———. "John Johnston & Co.: A Meeting of the Creditors." May 23, 1877. www.newspapers.com.

———. "John Johnston & Co.: On Application of the Assignees in the Bankruptcy Case of John Johnston & Co." May 29, 1878. www.newspapers.com.

———. "John Johnston & Co.: Some Facts in Regard to the Affairs of the Firm." July 9, 1877. www.newspapers.com.

———. "John Johnston & Co: The Suspension of this Banking Firm and Prospects for Creditors." May 14, 1877. www.newspapers.com.

———. "The Johnston Defalcation." February 21, 1878. www.newspapers.com.

———. "Meeting of Citizens Wednesday Morning: The Lexington and Bay City Project Put in Definitive Shape." February 22, 1872. www.newspapers.com.

———. "Mr. Bancroft's Report." December 21, 1875. www.newspapers.com.

———. "Political Meetings." October 16, 1872. www.newspapers.com.

———. "Railroads: Visit of the Saginaw Committee to this City." February 22, 1872. www.newspapers.com.

———. "Republican City Convention." March 29, 1872. www.newspapers.com.

———. "Resolution of Bankers." September 28, 1873. www.newspapers.com.

———. "Treasurer Issue." December 6, 1875. www.newspapers.com.

———. "Treasurer Issue." December 9, 1875. www.newspapers.com.

Rockoff, Hugh. "The Free Banking Era: A Reexamination." *Journal of Money, Credit and Banking* 6, no. 2 (May 1974): 141–67. https://www.jstor.org/stable/1991023.

Shutterstock. "Everett Collection. Financial Panic of 1873. Thomas Nast Cartoon Illustration." https://www.shutterstock.com/image-illustration/financial-panic-1873-thomas-nast-cartoon-242294134.

U.S. Department of Treasury. "Financial Panic of 1873." https://home.treasury.gov/about/history/freedmans-bank-building/financial-panic-of-1873.

Wickings, Elizabeth Isabell, and Erica Wickings (living descendants of Peter W. Reed, Robert H. Reed, Elizabeth Thacher Reed Isabell and Harvey Isabell). Interview of family members, Brenda L. Williams. Port Huron, MI. February 19, 2023.

Wickings, Erica. "The Charles A. Hammond American Legion Post 8: A Hidden History." Final paper, St. Clair County Community College, 2022.

Williams, Brenda L. "The 'Henry McMorran.'" Tappingroots. 2018. https://tappingroots.com/2018/09/23/the-henry-mcmorran/.

———. "Young Henry." Tappingroots. 2017. https://tappingroots.
com/2017/10/29/young-henry/.

Chapter 3

"An Act to Provide for the Formation of Companies for Running, Driving, Booming and Rafting Logs, Timber, and Lumber and for Regulating the Floatage Thereof." In *Acts of the Legislature of the State of Michigan Passed at the Regular Session of 1855.* Lansing, MI: Geo. W. Peck Printer to the State, 1855. Google Books. https://books.google.cd/books?id=OTs4AA AAIAAJ&printsec=frontcover&hl=fr&source=gbs_ge_summary_r&cad =0#v=onepage&q=booming%20companies&f=false.

Allen, Clifford, ed. "Michigan Log Marks." *Memoir Bulletin* (1941): 1–30. https://babel.hathitrust.org/cgi/pt?id=mdp.39015013152700&view=1 up&seq=1.

Ames v. Port Huron Log Driving & Booming Co., RG 2003-32. Michigan Supreme Court, Clerk's Office. Court calendars, volume 14, page 20, file no. 20, 1857. Michigan Supreme Court Records, Michigan State Archives.

Ames v. Port Huron Log Driving & Booming Co., RG 2003-32. Michigan Supreme Court, Clerk's Office. Court calendars, volume 14, page 448, file no. 448, 1862. Michigan Supreme Court Records, Michigan State Archives.

Ames v. Port Huron Log Driving & Booming Co., RG 96-169. Michigan Supreme Court, Clerk's Office. Case files, box 48, file no. 20, 1857. Michigan Supreme Court Records, Michigan State Archives.

Ames v. Port Huron Log Driving & Booming Co., RG 96-169. Michigan Supreme Court, Clerk's Office. Case files, box 69, file no. 448, 1862. Michigan Supreme Court Records, Michigan State Archives.

Ancestry. "Cummings Sanborn Estate File, Cal. 1, No. 268, *Probate Calendars and Estate Files, 1828–1902; Probate Index, 1838–1975; Author: Michigan. Probate Court (St. Clair County);* Probate Place*: St Clair, Michigan." Michigan, U.S., Wills and Probate Records, 1784–1980* [database on-line]. 2015. https://www.ancestry.com/discoveryui-content/ view/1481600:8793?_phsrc=FfJ860&_phstart=successSource&gsfn=cu mmings&gsln=sanborn&ml_rpos=1&queryId=93e398523c613c03bc7f 2c1f849c6c67.

Andreas, A.T. *History of St. Clair County, Michigan.* Chicago: A.T. Andreas and Co., 1883.

Bowling, Terra, and Madeline Doten. "Memorandum to Mary Bohling, Advisory Summary on the Access to Michigan Water Trails from Bridges." National Sea Grant Law Center, University of Mississippi School of Law. 2020. https://nsglc.olemiss.edu/Advisory/pdfs/watertrailaccess-mi.pdf.

Bureau of Land Management. "Abner Coburn Search Results List." GLO Records. https://glorecords.blm.gov/results/default.aspx?searchCriteria=type=patent|st=MI|cty=|ln=coburn|fn=abner|sp=true|sw=true|sadv=false.

———. "Aloney Rust Search Results List." GLO Records. https://glorecords.blm.gov/results/default.aspx?searchCriteria=type=patent|st=MI|cty=|ln=rust|fn=aloney|sp=true|sw=true|sadv=false.

———. "Alvah Sweetser Search Results List." GLO Records. https://glorecords.blm.gov/results/default.aspx?searchCriteria=type=patent|st=MI|cty=|ln=sweetser|fn=alvah|sp=true|sw=true|sadv=false.

———. "Charles Merrill Search Results List." GLO Records. https://glorecords.blm.gov/results/default.aspx?searchCriteria=type=patent|st=MI|cty=|ln=merrill|fn=charles|sp=true|sw=true|sadv=false.

———. "Cummings Sanborn Search Results List." GLO Records. https://glorecords.blm.gov/results/default.aspx?searchCriteria=type=patent|st=MI|cty=|ln=sanborn|fn=cummings|sp=true|sw=true|sadv=false.

———. "David Ward Search Results List." GLO Records. https://glorecords.blm.gov/results/default.aspx?searchCriteria=type=patent|st=MI|cty=|ln=ward|fn=david|sp=true|sw=true|sadv=false.

———. "James W. Sanborn Search Results List." GLO Records. https://glorecords.blm.gov/results/default.aspx?searchCriteria=type=patent|st=MI|cty=|ln=sanborn|fn=james|sp=true|sw=true|sadv=false.

———. "Thomas W. Palmer Search Results List." GLO Records. https://glorecords.blm.gov/results/default.aspx?searchCriteria=type=patent|st=MI|cty=|ln=palmer|fn=thomas|sp=true|sw=true|sadv=false.

"Chapter 164: Rafting and Booming Companies." In *The Compiled Laws of the State of Michigan*. Vol. 2. *Chapters 97–203*. Lansing, MI: Wynkoop, Hallenbeck, Crawford Co. State Printers, 1916. Google Books. https://www.google.com/books/edition/The_Compiled_Laws_of_the_State_of_Michig/QA9fUsYt-MgC?hl=en&gbpv=0.

Dasef, John W. *History of Montcalm County, Michigan*. Indianapolis: B.F. Bowen and Company Inc., 1916. Michigan County Histories and Atlases Digital Project. https://quod.lib.umich.edu/m/micounty/3933273.0001.001?view=toc.

Detroit Free Press. "The Income List: Full Rounds of the City and County." June 25, 1866. www.newspapers.com.

Farmer, Silas. *History of Detroit and Michigan*. Vol. 2. Illustrations by Charles Merrill and Stephen Moore. Detroit, MI: Silas Farmer and Co., 1889. Google Books. https://www.google.com/books/edition/The_History_ of_Detroit_and_Michigan/nEFSAAAAYAAJ?q=manchester+new+ha mpshire+franklin+moore&gbpv=0#f=false.

Harvard Law School. "*Ames v. Port Huron Log Driving & Booming Co.*, 6 Mich. 266; 1859 Mich. LEXIS 7." Caselaw Access Project. https://cite.case. law/mich/6/266/.

———. "*Ames v. Port Huron Log Driving & Booming Co.*, 11 Mich. 139; 1863 Mich. LEXIS 3." Caselaw Access Project. https://cite.case.law/ mich/11/139/.

———. "*Moore v. Sanborne, et al.*, 2 Mich. 519, Michigan Supreme Court, Jan. 1853." Caselaw Access Project. https://cite.case.law/mich/2/519/.

Hotchkiss, George Woodward. *History of the Lumber and Forest Industry of the Northwest*. Chicago: G.W. Hotchkiss and Company, 1898. Google Books. https://www.google.com/books/edition/History_of_the_ Lumber_and_Forest_Industr/U5c4AQAAMAAJ?hl=en&gbpv=1.

Jenks, William Lee. *St. Clair County, Michigan: Its History and Its People: A Narrative Account of Its Historical Progress and Its Principal Interests*. Vol. 1. New York: Lewis Publishing Company, 1912.

Journal of the Senate of the State of Michigan. Lansing, MI: Hosmer & Fitch Printers to the State, 1855. Hathitrust. https://babel.hathitrust.org/cgi/ pt?id=uc1.b2882129&view=1up&seq=5.

Leeson, Michael A. *History of Saginaw County, Michigan*. Chicago: C.C. Chapman and Co., 1881. Michigan County Histories and Atlases Digital Project. https://quod.lib.umich.edu/m/micounty/bad1164.000 1.001/572?rgn=full+text;view=image;q1=sanborn.

Library of Congress. "Omar D. Conger, Senator of Michigan between 1865–1880, [portrait]." https://www.loc.gov/resource/cwpbh.04949/.

Library of Michigan. "James W. Sanborn Profile." Michigan Legislative Biography. https://mdoe.state.mi.us/legislators/Legislator/ LegislatorDetail/76.

Meek, Forrest B. *Michigan's Timber Battleground: A History of Clare County: 1674–1900*. Clare County, MI: Published in conjunction with the Clare County Bicentennial Historical Committee, 1976. Clarke Historical Library Digital Collections. https://clarkedigitalcollections.cmich. edu/?a=d&d=Clarke1976-02.1.79&e=-------en-10--1--txt-txIN--------.

Michigan State University. "James W. Sanborn Log Mark, Paul Emmory Log Mark Collection, [photograph]." MSU Libraries, Digital Repository. https://d-legacy.lib.msu.edu/mmm/21579.

Mitts, Dorothy. "Famous Pine River 'Log' Lawsuit." *Port Huron Times Herald*, January 9, 1966. www.newspapers.com.

Moore v. Sanborne, et al., RG 2013-32. Michigan Supreme Court, Clerk's Office. Court case files box 51, file no. 148, Michigan Supreme Court Records, Michigan State Archives.

National Park Service. "Logging History." https://www.nps.gov/piro/learn/historyculture/logging-history.html.

Oakland County, Michigan. "Court History: Early Justice in Oakland County." https://www.oakgov.com/courts/circuit/resources/publications/Pages/court-history.aspx.

Port Huron Daily Times. "Daniel D. Runnels: Sketch of the Life of an Enterprising and Liberal Citizen Arguments Favoring the Renomination of the Present Register of Deeds." December 7, 1896. www.newspapers.com.

———. "Reception at Library Attended by Members of Common Council and Other City Boards on Wednesday Evening." December 15, 1904. www.newspapers.com.

Portrait & Biographical Album Mecosta County, Michigan. Chicago: Chapman Brothers, 1883. Michigan County Histories and Atlases Digital Project. https://quod.lib.umich.edu/m/micounty/bad0976.0001.001/7?rgn=full+text;view=image;q1=sanborn.

randymajor.org. "Section Township Range Locator for Section 7, Township 6N, Range 16E." https://www.randymajors.org/township-range-on-google-maps?x=-82.6123310&y=42.9684102&cx=-82.6117945&cy=42.9658194&zoom=16.

———. "Section Township Range Locator for Section 27, Township 6N, Range 16E." https://www.randymajors.org/township-range-on-google-maps?x=-82.5510747&y=42.9262413&cx=-82.5510747&cy=42.9262413&zoom=14.

Revised Constitution of the State of Michigan art. IV, §18. Lansing, MI: R.W. Ingals State Printer, 1850. Hathitrust. https://babel.hathitrust.org/cgi/pt?id=mdp.39015071174802&view=1up&seq=1.

Sanborn, V.C. *Genealogy of the Family of Samborne or Sanborn in England and America 1194–1898*. Illustrations by Cummings Sanborn and James W. Sanborn. La Grange, IL: Self-published, 1899.

Teaching Books. "Carnegie Libraries." 2017. https://www.teachingbooks.net/media/pdf/Owlkids/Carnegie_Facts-USA.pdf.

U.S. Department of the Interior, Bureau of Land Management. "Patent of Cummings Sanborn, Certificate No. 14111, East half of the Southwest quarter and the Northwest Quarter of the Southwest quarter, Section 27, Township 6N, Range 16E, 120 Acres, Issued April 10, 1837." www.glorecords.blm.gov.

———. "Patent of Franklin and Reuben Moore, Certificate No. 17071, Northeast Quarter Section Seven, Township 6N, Range 16E, Issued May 1, 160 Acres, 1837." www.glorecords.blm.gov.

Ward, David. *The Autobiography of David Ward.* New York: Privately printed, 1912. Google Books. https://www.google.com/books/edition/The_Autobiography_of_David_Ward/gE4vAAAAYAAJ?hl=en&gbpv=1&printsec=frontcover.

Wellman, Vincent A. "Some Remarks on Michigan's Reception of the Common Law." Michigan Supreme Court Historical Society. https://www.micourthistory.org/wp-content/uploads/2018/06/Wellman.pdf.

Wikipedia. "Charles Merrill." https://en.wikipedia.org/wiki/Charles_Merrill_(businessman).

———. "Joseph T. Copeland." https://en.wikipedia.org/wiki/Joseph_T._Copeland.

———. "Thomas W. Palmer." https://en.wikipedia.org/wiki/Thomas_W._Palmer.

———. "Zachariah Chandler." https://en.wikipedia.org/wiki/Zachariah_Chandler.

Williams, Charles Evarts. *The Life of Abner Coburn: A Review of the Public and Private Career of the Late Ex-Governor of Maine.* Bangor, ME: Press of Thomas W. Burr, 1885. Internet Archive. https://archive.org/details/lifeabnercoburn00willgoog/page/n8/mode/2up.

Chapter 4

"An Act to Provide for the Formation of Companies for Running, Driving, Booming and Rafting Logs, Timber, and Lumber and for Regulating the Floatage Thereof." In *Acts of the Legislature of the State of Michigan Passed at the Regular Session of 1855.* Lansing, MI: Geo. W. Peck Printer to the State, 1855. Google Books. https://books.google.cd/books?id=OTs4AAAAIAAJ&printsec=frontcover&hl=fr&source=gbs_ge_summary_r&cad=0#v=onepage&q=booming%20companies&f=false.

Ames v. Port Huron Log Driving & Booming Co., RG 2003-32. Michigan Supreme Court, Clerk's Office. Court calendars, volume 14, page 20, file no. 20, 1857. Michigan Supreme Court Records, Michigan State Archives.

Ames v. Port Huron Log Driving & Booming Co., RG 2003-32. Michigan Supreme Court, Clerk's Office. Court calendars, volume 14, page 448, file no. 448, 1862. Michigan Supreme Court Records, Michigan State Archives.

Ames v. Port Huron Log Driving & Booming Co., RG 96-169. Michigan Supreme Court, Clerk's Office. Case files, box 48, file no. 20, 1857. Michigan Supreme Court Records, Michigan State Archives.

Ames v. Port Huron Log Driving & Booming Co., RG 96-169. Michigan Supreme Court, Clerk's Office. Case files, box 69, file no. 448, 1862. Michigan Supreme Court Records, Michigan State Archives.

Andreas, A.T. *History of St. Clair County, Michigan.* Chicago: A.T. Andreas and Co., 1883.

Bergeron, Paul H. *The Papers of Andrew Johnson.* Vol. 12. *February–August 1867.* Knoxville: University of Tennessee Press, 1995. Google Books. https://www.google.com/books/edition/The_Papers_of_Andrew_Johnson/I1oo__8_XU8C?q=john+p+sanborn+us+customs+and+port+huron&gbpv=0#f=false.

Book Units Teacher. "The Civil War: The Compromises of 1820 and 1850." https://bookunitsteacher.com/civil_war/compromise_of_1850.htm.

Cooley, Thomas McIntyre. "Jonas H. Titus v. Minnesota Mining Co." In *Michigan Reports.* Vol. 8. Ann Arbor: Michigan Supreme Court, 1860. Google Books. https://www.google.com/books/edition/_/4V6NMQAKk7kC?hl=en&sa=X&ved=2ahUKEwilgevVlq_-AhU4kYkEHcNxC0YQ7_IDegQIDRAC.

Courter, Ellis W. "Michigan's Copper County." Michigan. https://www.michigan.gov/-/media/Project/Websites/egle/Documents/Programs/OGMD/Catalog/02/CMG92.PDF?rev=609c71b87a5c4b93a80469874aabbf34.

Detroit Free Press. "The Commissionership of the Land Office." September 8, 1858. www.newspapers.com.

———. "Notice." January 28, 1862. www.newspapers.com.

Everett Collection. "*The Civil War. John Brown's Raid on Harpers Ferry. Brown and Fellow Raiders Trapped in Engine House, Now Known as John Brown's Fort. Harpers Ferry Amory,* 1859." Shutterstock. https://www.shutterstock.com/image-illustration/civil-war-john-browns-raid-on-238815061.

————. "*A Pro-Slavery Mob Burning Down the Building Housing the Newspaper of Abolitionist Elijah Parish Lovejoy* (1802–1837)." Shutterstock. November 7, 1837. https://www.shutterstock.com/image-illustration/proslavery-mob-burning-down-building-housing-242301124.

Experience Jackson. "Under the Oaks." https://www.experiencejackson.com/business/under-the-oaks.

Fierst, John T. "Return to Civilization: John Tanner's Troubled Years at Sault Ste. Marie." Minnesota Historical Society. http://collections.mnhs.org/MNHistoryMagazine/articles/50/v50i01p023-036.pdf.

Gardner, Alexander. "*Planning the Capture of Booth* [photograph], 1865." Met Collection API, Metropolitan Museum of Art. https://www.metmuseum.org/art/collection/search/286617.

Henry R. Schoolcraft portrait. *Popular Science Monthly* 37 (May–October 1890). Library of Congress. https://www.loc.gov/item/93517606/.

Hudson Heritage Association. "Girl Scouts Underground Railroad Quest." https://hudsonheritage.org/girls-scouts-underground-railroad-quest/.

Hudson Library and Historical Society. "John Brown." Hudson Memory. https://www.hudsonmemory.org/people/john-brown/.

————. "Western Reserve College: One of the Earliest Institutions of Higher Learning in the Region, Once Called 'The Yale of the West.'" Hudson Memory. https://www.hudsonmemory.org/places/western-reserve-college/.

Journal of the Senate of the State of Michigan. Lansing, MI: Hosmer and Fitch Printers to the State, 1857. Google Books. https://www.google.com/books/edition/Journal/0j_iAAAAMAAJ?hl=en&gbpv=0.

Kansas City Public Library. "James Buchanan." Civil War on the Western Border. https://civilwaronthewesternborder.org/encyclopedia/buchanan-james.

Leonard, Maxine Crowell. *The Conger Family of America*. Author's ed. N.p.: Self-published, 1972.

Library of Congress. "Black, James Wallace & Lawrence, Martin M. John Brown. [photograph], c. 1859." https://www.loc.gov/resource/ppmsca.23763/.

————. "*Interior of Chief Detective Col. Baker's Office, Opposite Willard's Hotel, Washington, D.C.—Col. Baker Laying Down the Plan of Booth's Capture to His Chief Subordinates*, 1865." https://www.loc.gov/resource/cph.3a09606/.

————. "*Journal of the Senate of the United States of America*, April 12, 1866 and April 16, 1866." American Memory. https://memory.loc.gov/ammem/amlaw/lawhome.html.

————. "Omar Dwight Conger of Michigan, [portrait photograph], 1860–1875." https://www.loc.gov/resource/cwpbh.00327/.

————. "Timeline of the Civil War." https://www.loc.gov/collections/civil-war-glass-negatives/articles-and-essays/time-line-of-the-civil-war/1861/#:~:text=The%20secession%20of%20South%20Carolina,the%20Confederate%20States%20of%20America.

————. "Zachariah Chandler, 1855–1865." https://www.loc.gov/resource/cwpbh.02069/.

Library of Michigan. "James W. Sanborn Profile." Michigan Legislative Biography. https://mdoe.state.mi.us/legislators/Legislator/LegislatorDetail/76.

Livingston Republican. "Republican Congressional Convention—Fifth District." August 5, 1868. www.newspapers.com.

Lord, William Blair, and Brown, David Wolfe. *The Debates and Proceedings of the Constitutional Convention of the State of Michigan.* Vol. 2. Lansing, MI: John A. Kerr and Co. Printers to the State, 1867. Google Books. https://www.google.com/books/edition/The_Debates_and_Proceedings_of_the_Const/Ukm6F-UmeS0C?hl=en&gbpv=0.

Michigan. "Geological Survey of Michigan." https://www.michigan.gov/-/media/Project/Websites/egle/Documents/Programs/OGMD/Catalog/09/GIMDL-VOLIA.PDF?rev=f63660f67590492a8113e46ba8de670d.

National Archives. "Dred Scott v. Sanford (1857)." Milestone Documents. https://www.archives.gov/milestone-documents/dred-scott-v-sandford.

National Park Service. "Timeline of Michigan Copper Mining Prehistory to 1850." https://www.nps.gov/kewe/learn/historyculture/copper-mining-timeline.htm.

Ohio History Central. "Western Reserve College." Ohio History Connection. https://ohiohistorycentral.org/w/Western_Reserve_College#:~:text=Originally%20established%20at%20Hudson%2C%20Ohio,anti%2Dslavery%20sentiment%20in%20Ohio.

Port Huron Daily Times. "The Campaign—Speech of Hom. Omar D. Conger on Monday Evening." November 11, 1870. www.newspapers.com.

————. "The Customs House." April 7, 1883. www.newspapers.com.

Richardson, Heather Cox. *To Make Men Free: A History of the Republican Party.* New York: Basic Books, 2021.

Rubenstein, Bruce A. "Omar D. Conger: Michigan's Forgotten Favorite Son." *Michigan History Magazine* 66, no. 5 (September/October 1982): 32–39.

Sanborn, V.C. *Genealogy of the Family of Samborne or Sanborn in England and America 1194–1898*. La Grange, IL: Self-published, 1899.

Steere, Joseph H. "Sketch of John Tanner, Known as the 'White Indian.'" *Michigan Historical Collections* 22 (1894): 246–54.

Stocking, William, ed. *Under the Oaks: Commemorating the Fiftieth Anniversary of the Founding of the Republican Party, at Jackson, Michigan, July 6, 1854*. Detroit, MI: Detroit Tribune, 1904.

Thayer, George W. "From Vermont to Lake Superior in 1845: A Personal Narrative Delivered before the 'Old Residents Association' of the Grand River Valley, June 26, 1902." *Michigan Historical Collections* 30 (1906): 549–65.

United States Senate. "The Kansas-Nebraska Act." https://www. senate.gov/artandhistory/history/minute/Kansas_Nebraska_Act. htm#:~:text=It%20became%20law%20on%20May,territories%20 to%20sway%20the%20vote.

Weadock, Thomas A.E. "The Public Services of Hon. Sanford M. Green." *Michigan Historical Collections* 17 (1892): 364.

Wick, Rob. "Lincoln's Avenger: The Untold Story of Everton J. Conger." Roger J. Norton. https://rogerjnorton.com/Conger%20series%20 manuscript.pdf.

Wikipedia. "American Civil War." https://en.wikipedia.org/wiki/ American_Civil_War.

———. "Connecticut Western Reserve." https://en.wikipedia.org/wiki/ Connecticut_Western_Reserve.

———. "Daniel R. Tilden." https://en.wikipedia.org/wiki/Daniel_R._ Tilden.

———. "Douglass Houghton." https://en.wikipedia.org/wiki/Douglass_ Houghton.

———. "Elijah Parish Lovejoy." https://en.wikipedia.org/wiki/Elijah_ Parish_Lovejoy.

———. "Franklin Benjamin Sanborn." https://en.wikipedia.org/wiki/ Franklin_Benjamin_Sanborn.

———. "James Buchanan." https://en.wikipedia.org/wiki/James_Buchanan.

———. "John Brown's Raid on Harpers Ferry." https://en.wikipedia.org/ wiki/John_Brown%27s_raid_on_Harpers_Ferry#:~:text=John%20 Brown's%20raid%20on%20Harpers%20Ferry%20was%20an%20 effort%20by,since%201863%2C%20West%20Virginia).

———. "Omar D. Conger." https://en.wikipedia.org/wiki/Omar_D._Conger.

Woodcut of Western Reserve College, taken about 1860. General Photograph Collection, P.04.00.00777, Hudson Library and Historical Society.

Yale Expositor. "Omar D. Conger: Once the Pride of Our County and State Now Dead." July 15, 1898. www.newspapers.com.

Zachariah Chandler. Detroit, MI: Post and Tribune Company, 1880.

Chapter 5

Ancestry. "James Sanborn Estate File, Cal 2, No. 498, Cal. 2, No. 527 and Cal. 4, No. 9, *Probate Calendars and Estate Files, 1828–1902; Probate Index, 1838–1975*; Author*: Michigan. Probate Court (St. Clair County)*; Probate Place: *St Clair, Michigan." Michigan, U.S., Wills and Probate Records, 1784–1980* [database on-line]. 2015. https://www.ancestry.com/discoveryui-content/view/292214:8793?_phsrc=FfJ849&_phstart=successSource&gsfn=james&gsln=sanborn&ml_rpos=3&queryId=14b0a4863dab7a664b57f887e2302fd1.

Articles of Association of the Port Huron Railway Company. William Lee Jenks papers, 1779–1936. University of Michigan Library Special Collections, Ann Arbor, Michigan.

Everett Collection. "James G. Blaine, 1870s." Shutterstock. https://www.shutterstock.com/image-illustration/james-g-blaine-1870s-245964142.

———. "*Scene of the Assassination of Gen. James A. Garfield President of the United States by Charles J. Guiteau* [engraving], December 21, 1881." Shutterstock. https://www.shutterstock.com/image-illustration/scene-assassination-gen-james-garfield-president-238811374.

Harvard Law School. "*Sanborn v. Mitchell*, 94 Mich. 519; 1893." Caselaw Access Project. https://cite.case.law/mich/94/519/.

Jenks, William Lee. "History of the Port Huron Street Railways. William Lee Jenks Papers, 1779–1936. University of Michigan Library Special Collections, Ann Arbor, Michigan.

Library of Congress. "Haasis & Lubrecht. Our Nation's Choice. [lithograph], c. 1880." https://www.loc.gov/resource/pga.03269/.

———. "*Hon. Senator Omar Dwight Conger of Mich.* [portrait photograph], c. 1865–1880." Brady-Handy Photograph Collection. https://www.loc.gov/item/2017895222/.

Library of Michigan. "Byron Parks." Legislative Biography. https://mdoe.state.mi.us/legislators/Legislator/LegislatorDetail/2106.

———. "Edward Vincent." Legislative Biography. https://mdoe.state.mi.us/legislators/Legislator/LegislatorDetail/2120.

———. "Henry Meyer." Legislative Biography. https://mdoe.state.mi.us/legislators/Legislator/LegislatorDetail/2103.

————. "Justin Rice Whiting." Legislative Biography. https://mdoe.state.
mi.us/legislators/Legislator/LegislatorDetail/4646.

Los Angeles Times. "Detroit & Port Huron Shore Line Railway, East
Whittier: Another Promising Town in the Beautiful Los Angeles Valley."
December 31, 1887. www.newspapers.com.

————. "Hotel San Gabriel: A Picnic: The House Filling Up with
Summer Guests." www.newspapers.com.

————. "Incorporated." June 15, 1887. www.newspapers.com.

————. "Ramirez." August 23, 1887. www.newspapers.com.

Morphart Creation. "Roscoe Conkling, U.S. Senator from New York."
Shutterstock. https://www.shutterstock.com/image-vector/roscoe-
conkling-1829-1888-he-politician-1401446183.

PBS. "The Conkling Problem." American Experience. https://www.pbs.
org/wgbh/americanexperience/features/presidents-lying-garfield/.

Port Huron Daily Times, December 28, 1882. www.newspapers.com.

————. January 6, 1883. www.newspapers.com.

————. January 8, 1883. www.newspapers.com.

————. January 16, 1883. www.newspapers.com.

————. January 27, 1883. www.newspapers.com.

————. June 8, 1907. www.newspapers.com.

————. "The Anti-Grant Men Gain Their Point: Associated Press
Dispatches." June 2, 1880. www.newspapers.com.

————. "Arrangement of the Hall: The Republican Convention." June 3,
1880. www.newspapers.com.

————. "The Balloting Begins: Ferry Gets Fifty Nine Votes." January 16,
1883. www.newspapers.com.

————. "Comments and Speculations." June 3, 1880. www.newspapers.
com.

————. "Conkling." May 18, 1881. www.newspapers.com.

————. "Conkling's Chances." May 19, 1881. www.newspapers.com.

————. "A Conkling View." May 12, 1881. www.newspapers.com.

————. "The Custom House Controversy." January 24, 1883. www.
newspapers.com.

————. "The Custom House Controversy." January 31, 1883. www.
newspapers.com.

————. "The Custom House Controversy: Newspaper Comments on the
Candidates and the Controversy for the Collectorship." February 7,
1883. www.newspapers.com.

———. "The Custom House: Mr. John P. Sanborn Retires After Serving Four Years as Deputy Collector and Sixteen Years as Collector: Some Facts Regarding his Incumbency." April 7, 1883. www.newspapers.com.

———. "1880 Republican Ticket." June 22, 1880. www.newspapers.com.

———. "A Friend of President Garfield Commenting." May 4, 1881. www.newspapers.com.

———. "A Good Suggestion." May 8, 1880. www.newspapers.com.

———. "The High School." August 3, 1906. www.newspapers.com.

———. "An Interview with Mr. Conger: Chicago Tribune." Reprint. June 1, 1880, June 2, 1880. www.newspapers.com.

———. "John P. Sanborn." December 30, 1914. www.newspapers.com.

———. "Michigan News." June 2, 1880. www.newspapers.com.

———. "Mr. Conger." June 7, 1880. www.newspapers.com.

———. "Mrs. Garfield in a Critical Condition." May 13, 1881. www.newspapers.com.

———. "The New York Senators Resign." May 17, 1881. www.newspapers.com.

———. "Political History: Detroit News Repeats Story of Ancient Port Huron Contest." December 13, 1907. www.newspapers.com.

———. "The Republican Convention: General Garfield for President and General Arthur for Vice-President." June 9, 1880. www.newspapers.com.

———. "The Republican Convention: Proceedings Friday and Saturday Reported of the Committee on Credentials in Full." June 5, 1880. www.newspapers.com.

———. "The Republican Convention: The Preliminaries for the National Convention Completed." June 2, 1880. www.newspapers.com.

———. "Republican State Convention." April 23, 1884. www.newspapers.com.

———. "The Robertson Programme." May 16, 1881. www.newspapers.com.

———. "The Sanborn House Will be used for High School Purposes." July 21, 1906. www.newspapers.com.

———. "Senator Chandler: The Funeral at Detroit." November 6, 1879. www.newspapers.com.

———. "Senator Conger." January 6, 1881. www.newspapers.com.

———. "Senator Conger: His Speech on the Questions of Holiday Recess and Civil Service Reform." December 28, 1882. www.newspapers.com.

———. "The Senatorial Contest: A Great Crowd at Lansing Monday." January 16, 1883. www.newspapers.com.

———. "The Senatorial Contest: No Change in the Situation." January 20, 1883. www.newspapers.com.

———. "The Senatorial Contest: Rumors of Greenback Help for Ferry." January 24, 1883. www.newspapers.com.

———. "The Senatorial Contest: With a Loss of Six Votes to Mr. Ferry." January 19, 1883. www.newspapers.com.

———. "Senatorial: Omar D. Conger Nominated for Senator by the Republican Legislative Caucus." January 6, 1881. www.newspapers.com.

———. "Summary of the Week." May 4, 1881. www.newspapers.com.

———. "Supreme Court Decisions: Two Interesting Decisions Delivered to Clerk Today." January 13, 1894. www.newspapers.com.

———. "Washington News." December 2, 1882. www.newspapers.com.

———. "Washington News." December 8, 1882. www.newspapers.com.

———. "Washington News." December 11, 1882. www.newspapers.com.

———. "Washington News." December 22, 1882. www.newspapers.com.

———. "Washington News: The Caucus." May 10, 1881. www.newspapers.com.

———. "Washington News: Why They Did It." May 7, 1881. www.newspapers.com.

———. "The Wind Up of the Sanborn Estate Must be Effected and All of Its Real Estate Holdings Are Offered." August 30, 1912. www.newspapers.com.

Port Huron Times Herald. "Promoter Relates History of Local Electric Railway: Was First in Country One of the Original Owners Claim." December 20, 1929. www.newspapers.com.

Richardson, James D. *Messages and Papers of the Presidents*. Vol. 8. *James A. Garfield*. Washington, D.C.: Government Printing Office, 1897. Project Gutenburg. https://www.gutenberg.org/files/12318/12318.txt.

Sanborn, V.C. *Genealogy of the Family of Samborne or Sanborn in England and America 1194–1898*. La Grange, IL: Self-published, 1899.

Speller, John. "Detroit & Port Huron Shore Line Railway." Spellerweb. www.spellerweb.net.

Wikipedia. "Alexander Hamilton U.S. Custom House." https://en.wikipedia.org/wiki/Alexander_Hamilton_U.S._Custom_House.

———. "Assassination of James A. Garfield." https://en.wikipedia.org/wiki/Assassination_of_James_A._Garfield.

———. "Charles Merrill." https://en.wikipedia.org/wiki/Charles_Merrill_(businessman).

———. "Civil Service Reform in the United States." https://en.wikipedia. org/wiki/Civil_service_reform_in_the_United_States.

———. "1876 United States Presidential Election." https://en.wikipedia. org/wiki/1876_United_States_presidential_election.

———. "1880 Republican National Convention." https://en.wikipedia. org/wiki/1880_Republican_National_Convention.

———. "1880 United States Presidential Election." https://en.wikipedia. org/wiki/1880_United_States_presidential_election.

———. "1884 United States Presidential Election." https://en.wikipedia. org/wiki/1884_United_States_presidential_election.

———. "James Frederick Joy." https://en.wikipedia.org/wiki/James_ Frederick_Joy.

———. "James G. Blaine." https://en.wikipedia.org/wiki/James_G._Blaine.

———. "Pendleton Civil Service Reform Act." https://en.wikipedia.org/ wiki/Pendleton_Civil_Service_Reform_Act.

———. "Thomas W. Palmer." https://en.wikipedia.org/wiki/ Thomas_W._Palmer.

Williams, Brenda W. "The 'Henry McMorran." Tappingroots. https:// tappingroots.com/2018/09/23/the-henry-mcmorran/.

Ziewacz, Lawrence E. "The Eighty-First Ballot: The Senatorial Struggle of 1883." *Michigan History Magazine* 56, no. 3 (September 1972): 216–32.

ABOUT THE AUTHOR

Brenda L. Williams is the Director and Law Librarian at the Montgomery County Law Library in Dayton, Ohio. She was born and raised in Port Huron, Michigan. She is a graduate of St. Clair County Community College (Associate of Arts), American Public University (Bachelor of Science, Paralegal Studies) and San Jose State University (Master of Library and Information Science). She is the mother of three beautiful children, Matt, Emily and Miles. She is passionate about her friends and family, genealogy, research and writing. Brenda is a member of the Detroit Society for Genealogical Research, St. Clair County Genealogy and History Society and Harsens Island Historical Society. To read more of her historical writings, please visit her blog, www.tappingroots.com.